CONTENTS

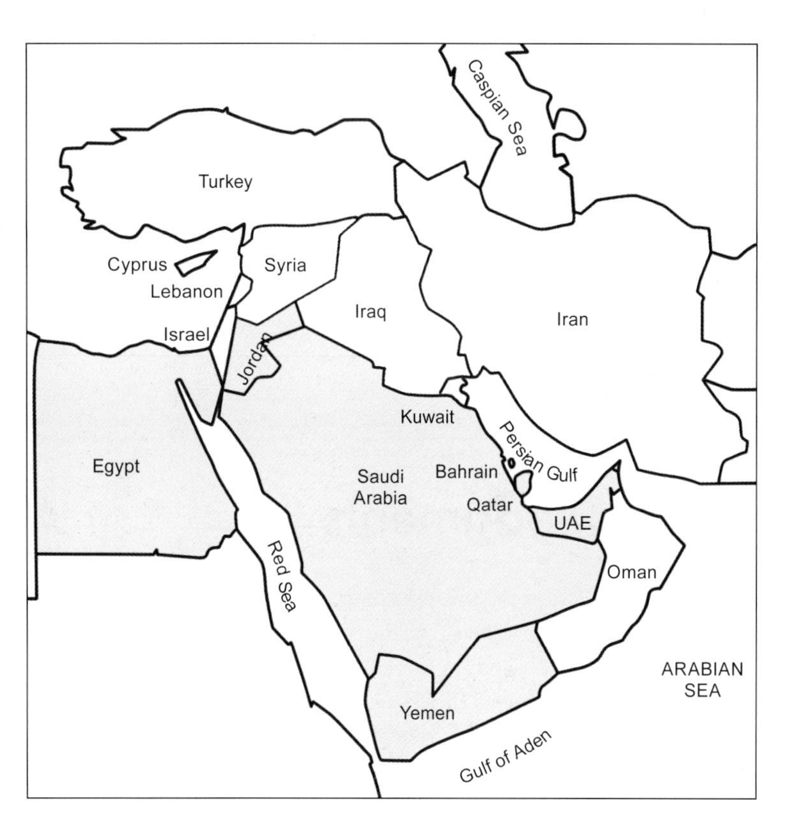

Helion & Company Limited
Unit 8 Amherst Business Centre
Budbrooke Road
Warwick
CV34 5WE
England
Tel. 01926 499 619
Fax 0121 711 4075
Email: info@helion.co.uk
Website: www.helion.co.uk
Twitter: @helionbooks
Visit our blog http://blog.helion.co.uk/

Published by Helion & Company 2018
Designed and typeset by Mach 3 Solutions Ltd (www.mach3solutions.co.uk)
Cover designed by Paul Hewitt, Battlefield Design (www.battlefield-design.co.uk)
Printed by Henry Ling Limited, Dorchester, Dorset

ISBN 978-1-911628-18-7

British Library Cataloguing-in-Publication Data.
A catalogue record for this book is available from the British Library.

Cover Image

A pair of F-5Es of the Yemen Air Force, seen underway north of Sana'a, in the early 2000s. (© Tom Cooper)

Note

In order to simplify the use of this book, all names, locations and geographic designations are as provided in *The Times World Atlas*, or other traditionally accepted major sources of reference, as of the time of the events described. Arabic names are romanised and transcripted rather than transliterated. For example: the definite article al- before words starting with 'sun letters' is given as pronounced instead of simply as al- (which is the usual practice for non-Arabic speakers in most English-language literature and media). For reasons of simplicity, genuine designations for Soviet/Russian-made weapons used in this book are mentioned once, and then their ASCC (or 'NATO') codes are used instead.

Acknowledgments

I would like to express my special thanks to a number of military-aviation researchers, analysts, and enthusiasts that helped me collect thousands of bits and pieces of the giant puzzle that eventually resulted in this book. Foremost amongst them are a number of contacts in Yemen, Saudi Arabia, and USA, that contributed a wealth of precious information about latest military-related developments on condition of anonymity. David Nicolle, from Great Britain, helped introduce me to the world of research about Arab military history, and is always supportive and encouraging of my work. His immense knowledge and in-depth understanding of local affairs are a lasting inspiration. I can never thank enough to Pit Weinert from Germany, whose research not only resulted in the contribution of his exclusive photographic collection, but also a number of largely unknown, yet precious articles published in the Yemeni press over time. Thanks to Stefan Knipschield from Germany, Mohammed Khalid from Saudi Arabia greatly enhanced the looks of this book by providing an amazing collection of exclusive photographs of aircraft of the Saudi-led coalition involved in the ongoing combat operations over Yemen, either taken by Fahd Rihan, or by Ahmed Hader, or officially released by the Ministry of Defence of Saudi Arabia. Albert Grandolini from France greatly encouraged this project and supported it with all his powers, his immense knowledge, and his photographic collection. Ali Tobchi from Iraq helped with additional articles and endless patience while translating materials available in the Arabic language only. Dmitry Zubkov helped with rare details sourced from specialised Russian literature, while Jeroen Nijmeijer and Menno van der Wal from The Netherlands provided precious details about unit designations and aircraft of Yemeni air forces. Last, but not least, I owe to express my gratitude to a number of visitors of the ACIG.info forum that contributed additional information over the years. This book would be literally impossible to prepare without help from all of them.

Abbreviations

AB	air base
ASOC	Air Support Operations Centre (RSAF)
An	Antonov (the design bureau led by Oleg Antonov)
AQAP	al-Qaeda in Arabian Peninsula
ASCC	Air Standardisation Coordinating Committee (NATO body responsible for issuing codes for foreign aircraft and weapons systems; designations for Soviet/Russian aircraft and weapons systems issued by this body are colloquially known as 'NATO codes')
CASEVAC	casualty evacuation
CIA	Central Intelligence Agency (USA)
C-in-C	commander in chief
c/n	construction number
CO	commanding officer
CSAR	combat search and rescue
CSF	Central Security Force (para-military force responsible for riot control and the protection of foreign embassies and officials since 1980s)
DHC	de Havilland Canada
EAF	Egyptian Air Force (official designation since 1972)
ELINT	electronic intelligence
FOIA	Freedom of Information Act (law in the USA)
FRA	Federal Regular Army
FSA	Federation of Southern Arabia
GPC	General People's Congress
HC	Hadramawt Confederation
HTC	Hadramawt Tribal Confederation
IDF	Israeli Defence Force
IDF/AF	Israeli Defence Force/Air Force
IED	Improvised Explosive Device
Il	Ilyushin (the design bureau led by Sergey Vladimirovich Ilyushin, also known as OKB-39)
IIAF	Imperial Iranian Air Force
IrAF	Iraqi Air Force
JMP	Joint Meeting Parties
KAF	Kuwait Air Force
LAL	Local Area Leader/s (Houthis)

MBG	Missile Brigades/Batteries Group (Yemen Army)
MiG	Mikoyan i Gurevich (the design bureau led by Artyom Ivanovich Mikoyan and Mikhail Iosifovich Gurevich, also known as OKB-155 or MMZ 'Zenit')
MRLS	multiple rocket launch system
NDF	National Democratic Front
NOGIMS	National Organization for General Intelligence and Military Security
NSO	National Security Organization (top intelligence and security agency in Yemen since 1980s)
PDRY	People's Democratic Republic of Yemen (South Yemen)
PDRYAF	People's Democratic Republic of Yemen Air Force (South Yemen, 1967-1994)
PGM	precision guided munition (guided bombs and missiles)
QEAF	Qatar Emiri Air Force
RAF	Royal Air Force (of the United Kingdom)
RBAF	Royal Bahraini Air Force
RJAF	Royal Jordanian Air Force
RSAF	Royal Saudi Air Force
RSBG	Royal Saudi Border Guards
RSLF	Royal Saudi Land Forces
RSN	Royal Saudi Navy
SAAF	South Arabia Air Force
SAM	surface-to-air missile
SIGINT	signals intelligence
SSC	Supreme Security Council (Houthi/Saleh coalition)
Su	Sukhoi (the design bureau led by Pavel Ossipovich Sukhoi, also known as OKB-51)
TFS	Tactical Fighter Squadron
UAE	United Arab Emirates
UAEAF	United Arab Emirates Air Force
UAR	United Arab Republic (Union of Egypt and Syria, 1959-1961)
UARAF	United Arab Republic Air Force (official EAF title from 1958 until 1972)
UNF	United National Front
UAV	unmanned (or uninhabited) aerial vehicle
USA	United States of America
USAF	United States Air Force
USSR	Union of Soviet Socialist Republics (also 'Soviet Union')
YAF	Yemen Air Force (since 1994)
Yak	Yakovlev (the design bureau led by Alexander Sergeyevich Yakovlev, also known as the JSC A. S. Yakovlev Design Bureau)
YAR	Yemen Arab Republic
YARAF	Yemen Arab Republic Air Force (North Yemen, 1967-1994)
YNA	Yemen National Army (since 2015)
YSP	Yemen Socialist Party

Addenda/Errata to Hot Skies over Yemen, Volume 1

Chapter 2, Yemen Civil War, 1962-1967, sub-chapter 'Air Combats'

In reaction to the publishing of Volume 1, Hadrian Jeffs from the UK provided the following information about a clash between Hawker Hunters of the Royal Air Force (RAF) and aircraft of the Egyptian air force (officially the 'United Arab Republic Air Force, UARAF, as of 1958-1972) over Yemen. Correspondingly, at an unknown date in 1966, a squadron leader from No. 1 Squadron, RAF (this unit was on a temporary deployment from RAF West Raynham to RAF Khorkamsar), intercepted a 'Russian-piloted MiG in Egyptian colours' when this cut through the airspace of Aden Protectorate on return from an air strike on an insurgent camp. The pilot of the Hawker Hunter FGA.Mk 9 scored multiple hits with his 30mm ADEN cannons, but the 'Russian pilot' managed to escape into the Yemeni airspace. Correspondingly, the British pilot was not credited with a kill. No Egyptian reports on this clash are known.

Chapter 2, Yemen Civil War, 1962-1967, sub-chapter 'Final Escalation'

Visitors of the ACIG.info forum – including Dmitry Zubkov and Jeroen Nijemeijer – drew the author's attention to several publications indicating that Egypt began receiving Tupolev Tu-16 bombers at a much earlier date than reported in Volume 1. According to Oleg Teterin's book 'In Egypt and in Zanzibar', published in 2011 in Russian, the first 12 Tu-16s reached Egypt by 6 November 1961. Correspondingly, Anatoly Nikolayevich Ivanov, one of the Soviet military interpreters involved in delivery of these bombers to the UARAF, recalled:

> In the fall of 1961, a team of translators had gathered for a 10-month assignment. We were told that in Cairo we would help convert Egyptian crews [*to Tu-16s; author's note*]. Captain Barannikov, who was already familiar to us, provided us with several lessons and recommended, first and foremost, to memorize the registration numbers of Tu-16s. These remained in my memory until today, as follws: ABN-75508 (more precisely: Alpha-Bravo-November 75508). We were to use these for contacting flight control in Belgrade, then Athens and Cairo while crossing borders and entering and leaving their control zones.
>
> ...we left Bila Tserkva on 6 November 1961. We made a refuelling stop in Budapest and spent the night there. The next morning, our squadron – consisting of 12 Tu-16s – took a course for Cairo. We quietly overflew Yugoslavia and then Greece. Whether by accident or design, we passed directly above an American military base located near Athens. Several fighters scrambled from there and they harassed us for longer, demanding us to land.
>
> Finally, we saw the African coast, Nile Delta, Alexandria, Sahara Desert. Shortly before the noon, we landed at Cairo West Air Base, where we were expected by the Soviet

> Ambassador to Egypt, V. Erofeev, our Defence Attaché and a group of chief engineers and other specialists. Egyptian dignitaries were there too, including Vice-President Anwar el-Sadat, Deputy Commander-in-Chief of the Egyptian Air Forces of Egypt, Field Marshal Abdel Hakim Amer, Chief-of-Staff of the Egyptian Army General Mohammed Fawzi, Commander-in-Chief of the air force, Mahmmoud Sidki Mahmoud and others.[1]

Such recollections are supported by other, independent sources. For example, document 'The Arab-Israeli Situation', from 6 December 1961, released by the Electronic Reading Room of the Central Intelligence Agency (henceforth 'CIA/FOIA/ERR'), cites on page 15:

> ...under terms of a recently concluded agreement with the Soviet Union, the UAR will receive the Tu-16 (Badger) aircraft which can carry a 10,000 pound payload to a combat radius of 1,650 nautical miles.

British military intelligence followed in fashion. Citing the 'Annual Report on the Armed Forces of the United Arab Republic for the year 1962', from 29 January 1963, Foreign Office 371/172937, PRO, Jesse Ferris summarized in his book 'Nasser's Gamble: How Intervention in Yemen Caused the Six-Day War and the Decline of Egyptian Power':

> Another area of close cooperation encompassed the top-secret Tu-16 bombing missions over Yemen and southern Saudi Arabia. As Egyptian pilots were still training on the Tu-16 when the intervention [in Yemen; author's note] began, they probably continued their instruction with live ammunition over Yemen. By the beginning of 1963, two squadrons of Tu-16s were stationed at Cairo West airport.

Further citing Ivanov, Teterin added these details:

> ...In summer of 1962, 15 additional Tu-16s were transferred to Egypt. ...Around the same time, the first six Antonov An-12 transports were delivered... Their arrival radically changed the role of airborne troops, who now turned into one of most powerful levels of Cairo's geopolitical influence in the Arab World. An-12s and paratroopers saw widespread deployment during the war in Yemen
>
> ...Except for us, there was another group of Soviet advisors in Egypt: they were teaching Egyptian pilots how to fly MiG-21F-13s and MiG-21PFs. Their primary task was the defence of possible Israeli air attacks on Cairo, Alexandria, and the Aswan hydroelectric power station...later I was sent to Ismailia, the third largest city in Egypt, located directly on the Suez Canal... where I was assigned to the Command of the Eastern District (of the United Arab Republic Air Force)....
>
> During our stay in the UAR, Egyptian military aircraft wore markings adopted in 1958, following the merger with Syria. This consisted of red, white, and black, with two little green stars on the white field. These roundels were applied symmetrically on the wing and fuselage. A big flag of the UAR was applied on the fin. Black, four-digit numbers in Arabic numerals were placed on the nose of the fuselage, in front of the headlight. Serials were applied to all UARAF aircraft and once assigned were never changed for the duration of service. It is worth noting that this system proved very useful for Israeli intelligence during the Arab-Israeli wars: it helped them monitor the strength and deployment of Egyptian aircraft.
>
> ...The aircraft wore no camouflage colours, but retained their bare metal colour. Egyptians were reluctant to repaint their aircraft in sand colour, explaining this would rapidly fade due to the sun. Similarly, the recommendation of our experts for them to construct shelters and create mock positions for aircraft met little enthusiasm: while agreeing with our experts, the Egyptians were in no hurry to take corresponding action.[2]

According to the same, and two other Russian publications, it was around the same time that Hosni Mubarak, future President of Egypt, became involved in Egyptian Tu-16 program. Mubarak converted to Ilyushin Il-28 light bombers at the Kant AB, in 1959. Two years later he underwent a four-month conversion course on Tu-16s at Ryazan AB, as a member of a team of four Egyptian crews, including a total of 10 pilots, navigators, radio operators and gunners. According to retired Soviet radio operator, Colonel E. A. Aslanov, following his first tour on Tu-16s in Yemen, in the period 1962-1973 Mubarak underwent a staff course at the Frunze Military Academy in Moscow, from March 1964 until April 1965.[3]

According to the same source, Egyptian Tu-16s were already flying combat sorties over Yemen by that date:

> From October 1962 to April 1963 I was on a special mission in the United Arab Republic Egypt. I participated in acts of war providing international aid to the Yemeni Republic. The crews of the regiment, together with crews of the UAR, performed combat flights on Tu-16 aircraft... I completed more than thirty sorties.

Ivanov specified that it was Tu-16s from the 244 Bomber Regiment, 56. 'Bereslavskoy' Aviation Division, that flew air strikes on targets in Yemen, by night, between October 1962 and February 1963, and that he met Mubarak at Hudaydah Air Base (AB) in Yemen, while this was in command of a Tu-16 squadron deployed there in 1964.[4]

Further in relation to Soviet flying operations over Yemen in this period, Teterin specified that the Soviet Union officially recognized the new government in Sana'a on 1 October 1962; however, Moscow began providing military assistance a week before. Only a day after the coup of 27 September 1962, and at the request of the Egyptian government, Soviets organized an air bridge between Cairo, Sana'a and Hudaydah. The first two aircraft – both operated by the 12th Guards Military Transport Aviation Division from Tula – flew from Cairo via Aswan to Sana'a on the evening of 28 September. Their cargo consisted of 43 barrels of kerosene (necessary for their flight back to Egypt), several tonnes of ammunition, an Egyptian delegation and a platoon of Egyptian paratroopers each. Additional Egyptian soldiers were deployed by An-12s to Sana'a and Tai'z during the night of 29 September.

Recovery of the 1970s

Post-Civil War recovery of Northern Yemen proved extremely problematic. In a country damaged by years of fighting and with an economy in tatters, the military ate up to 50% of the national budget, which totalled only some US$ 9 million. The Yemen Arab Republic (YAR) and its Yemen Arab Republic Air Force (YARAF) went through a period of internal unrest, interrupted only during the short war against South Yemen, fought in 1972.

Meanwhile, the Soviet Union proved keen to cooperate with the radical Marxist government in Aden: it not only ceased providing support to Sana'a, but deployed a large team of advisors the PDRY, where – combined with donations of combat aircraft – a small, but well-trained air force and army came into being. The People's Democratic Republic of Yemen Air Force (PDRYAF) became involved in several border clashes with Saudi Arabia through the early 1970s: it saw no action against British and Omani forces during the civil war in the latter country, but had a squadron of its aircraft and pilots deployed to Ethiopia during the Ogaden War of 1978.

In the mid-1970s, the YAR experienced a relatively short period of stability and economic development under the rule of leftist Colonel al-Hamidi, but then had its government hit by a series of assassinations. Eventually, Saudi favourite, Colonel Ali Abdullah Saleh al-Sanhani al-Humairi climbed to power in 1978. However, the development of the North Yemeni military was meanwhile lagging massively behind that of its southern neighbour. South Yemen went through several years of political stability and thus continued its military build-up. By 1979, the PDRYAF was a well-developed force with nearly 200 combat aircraft and helicopters organized into six regiments.

A major power struggle and rivalries between politicians in Aden of 1978, eventually resulted in the PDRY launching an invasion of North Yemen in February 1979. In the course of a month-long war, the Southerners scored a clear-cut victory, but refrained from removing the government in Sana'a. This short but bitter conflict resulted in both Yemeni governments placing huge orders for additional arms: Sana'a concluded a deal for Northrop F-5E Tiger II fighter-bombers sponsored by Saudi Arabia, but also placed an order for MiG-21s and Sukhoi Su-22s in the USSR. Aden

South Yemeni troops with 37mm M1939 flak of Chinese origin. (Pit Weinert Collection)

A MiG-17 (without suffix) of the South Yemeni air force, as seen in the mid-1970s. The second batch of these aircraft was painted in Light Admiralty Grey overall, and wore big serials (205 in this case) on front fuselages. Most of these aircraft eventually ended in Ethiopia, in 1977, where they were operated exclusively by Cuban crews. (Pit Weinert Collection)

One of a three An-26s acquired by South Yemen in late 1979, and operated by the Aden-based Transport Regiment. (Albert Grandolini Collection)

Pilots and ground crews of Su-22 equipped and Aden-based 22nd Attack Regiment of the South Yemeni Air Force, as seen in the mid-1980s. This was a relatively 'happy' period for this military service, during which it reached the peak of its effectiveness and preparedness. (Pit Weinert Collection)

North Yemen obtained only one An-26, and this wore a rather unusual camouflage pattern, apparently consisting of light sand and olive green colour on the top surfaces and sides, and light admiralty grey on undersurfaces. (Albert Grandolini Collection)

continued purchasing MiGs and Sukhois through most of the 1980s. Most of the expensive acquisitions and intensive training of the PDRYAF were destroyed in a single blow when, following another power struggle in Aden, a short civil war erupted in Southern Yemen in January 1986. In the course of air strikes, up to 75% of the air force was destroyed and the country weakened to the point where its new government was left with little option but to open intensive negotiations for a union with North Yemen. When related talks reached an advanced stage, the Republic of Yemen was declared on 22 May 1990: Saleh become the President, with Southerner Ali Salim al-Beidh as Vice-President. For the first time in centuries, Greater Yemen was finally united.

The Union of 1990 and the Civil War of 1994

The unification included a complex process that was to last over 30 months. While a unified Parliament was formed, a unity constitution agreed upon, and general elections held in April 1993, the rest of this effort largely failed, leaving Southerners feeling economically marginalized and often exposed to the violence of Northerners. Amongst related agreements, the two militaries were to merge, and a southerner was appointed the Minister of Defence. However, this post held no real authority because Saleh-loyalists controlled all of the important command positions.

Mistreated by the government in Sana'a, Beidh and his military commanders decided to force Saleh into serious negotiations through military action. On the morning of 4 May 1994, they unleashed the PDRYAF into air strikes on YARAF's air bases, and then into attacks on major political and economic installations. While falling well short of winning the war or taking the enemy by surprise, this effort did inflict significant damage. Not only that Saleh's official residence was hit, but both power stations providing electricity to the North Yemeni capital were knocked out.[11]

Gunners of the North Yemeni army in the process of firing their 122mm D-30 howitzer (of Soviet design), during the 1994 Civil War in Yemen. (Albert Grandolini Collection)

South Yemeni MiG-21UM two-seat conversion trainer, as seen at Aden AB in the late 1980s. Notable is not only the three-colour camouflage pattern, but also the national marking applied in a rather unusual position – on the front fuselage, right in front of the serial '134' (applied in red, as usual). (Albert Grandolini Collection)

Sana'a reacted with air strikes and attacks of surface-to-surface missile against Aden, but generally concentrated on winning the battle on the ground. In the course of two weeks of bitter battles, it not only destroyed major South Yemeni units deployed inside North Yemen, but also captured the Anad AB, north of Aden.

The Southerners retaliated by subjecting Sana'a to additional attacks with surface-to-surface missiles, but to no avail: By 27 May 1994, four major concentrations of the North Yemeni Army, reinforced by thousands of tribal militiamen, converged upon Aden and put the town under siege: instead of assaulting the city, they continued subjecting it to frequent artillery barrages for most of the following month.

The final collapse of the PDRY came rather suddenly. After all attempts at a negotiated settlement failed, and let down by local tribal leaders, Ali Salim al-Baidh fled abroad on 30 June 1994. Behind him, what was left of the Southern military fell apart: Aden AB and then Riyan AB were overrun by Northerners, knocking what was left of the PDRYAF out of battle. With this, most of the military gave up fighting: thousands of South Yemeni civilians and military personnel fled abroad.

Saudi Factor

The Kingdom of Saudi Arabia nowadays dominates the entire Arab World. It is not only the second-largest nation in this hemisphere (after Algeria), but foremost the spiritual home of the Muslim faith, a powerhouse and a dominant military power.

The history of Saudi Arabia is closely tied to that of Wahhabism – an ultra-conservative, radical and militant interpretation of Sunni Islam. Insisting on strict religious purity, this teaching emphases doctrines and practices that are supposedly linked to early Islam. Often mis-declared as 'Salafism' (despite significant differences between these two sects), Wahhabism was initiated by Muhammad Ibn Abd al-Wahhab from Nejd in the 18th Century. Wahhab was strongly influenced by the Koranic literalism of Ahmad Ibn Hanbal (who felt that Islam was overrun by corruption, superstition and existentialism), and by the teachings of the Islamic law scholar Taqi ad-Din Ahmad Ibn Taymiyya of the Medieval ages. Ibn Taymiyya's teachings were coloured by Crusader expeditions and the destruction of the Islamic Empire by the Mongol invasions. He concluded that the reasons for the collapse of this empire were authorities and political leaders who had failed to uphold the 'correct' ideals of Islam, and demanded 'true' Moslems to revolt against those leaders, and help establish a 'proper' Islamic state. Following that example, Wahhab's teachings became so intolerant that he was forced to flee from one place to the other before, in 1740, he found refuge in Diriyah, near Riyadh, which at that time was under the control of Muhammad Ibn Saud. Saud embraced Wahhab's ideas and they reached an agreement according to which the later was to implement and enforce such teachings in exchange for Wahhab's recognition of Saud as the leader of the movement.

For the following 140 years, the two families worked closely together to wage a series of invasions in the course of which they established themselves in control of the regions of Hejaz, Nejd, al-Hasa and took the province of Asir from the then Imamate of Yemen in the 1920s. The Kingdom of Saudi Arabia was founded in 1932, as an absolute monarchy, nominally governed along Islamic lines with Wahhabism as a state religion, and indoctrinated in schools. Nevertheless, this movement began distancing itself from the Saud royal family during the late 1950s and through the early 1960s, until the June 1967 Arab-Israeli War, when – intent on countering Israel – Saudi royals launched a campaign of spreading Wahhabism outside the country. Their idea was that, if what they perceived as a 'small Jewish force, leaning on religious cohesion, can defeat massive Arab militaries', then Arabs must be capable of developing a similar military force based on their own religion. Correspondingly, and using their oil wealth, the Saudis began establishing a network of charitable organizations and financing the development of mosques and religious schools where a new generation of young, religiously motivated fighters was indoctrinated. In this fashion, Taymiyya's and Wahhab's teachings became strongly influential for the emergence of modern-day fundamentalist and radical Islamist movement around the World.[12]

Because Saudi Arabia is the key oil supplier on the international market, the involvement of various cliques from within, or with links to, the royal family in the spread of extremist Islam and support for terrorist groups meanwhile active anywhere between Nigeria and the Philippines remained completely ignored on the international scene for most of the last 40 years. Although 14 out of 19 terrorists involved in attacks that killed nearly 3,000 in the USA of 11 September 2001, were Saudi citizens, Washington did amazingly little to prosecute their supporters in Saudi Arabia.

It was only in the late 2000s that the government in Riyadh started taking steps against Saudi-sourced sponsoring and the involvement of dozens of thousands of Saudi nationals in the emergence of quasi-Islamist para-states in different spots of the Middle East, Asia and Africa – and thus Yemen too – only once these became a clear threat for its very existence. Although drastically changing its stance towards such groups ever since, this proved much too late to save the public image of Saudi Arabia in the West: nowadays, the country is facing more severe accusations for violations of human rights and support of international terrorism than ever before. Indeed, it is widely perceived as 'ruled by a terrorist-supporting regime' by the Western public, although its government enjoys the widespread support of Western governments. At the same time, Saudi meddling and direct and indirect influence in Yemen since 1970s, is still entirely ignored.

Saudi Arabia became involved in Yemen in 1962, when the British Government convinced the government in Riyadh to start supporting the Royalists in response to the Egyptian-supported coup against Imam in Sa'ada. Always careful to keep the USA out of what they saw as their own sphere of interest, the Saudis have ever since developed an extensive network of patronage and influence in Yemen. While this provided them with an unrivalled understanding of the function of political affairs in the country, it also made them responsible for many of major developments in Yemen since mid-1970s.

CHAPTER 2
SA'ADA WARS

With Saleh in control over Sana'a and Aden, and without any foreign enemies, the unified Yemen entered a relatively peaceful period that was to last nearly ten years. During the reorganization of the late 1990s, the military not only integrated selected remnants of the former army of South Yemen, but was also re-oriented towards the protection of the government and defence from domestic, rather than outside, threats. Ground forces were reformed within five regional commands, including 8 armoured brigades, 16 infantry brigades, 6 mechanised brigades, 2 airborne/commando and 1 special forces brigades, 4 artillery brigades (three of these equipped with surface-to-surface missiles), and six air defence brigades. However, more than ever before, officers from Saleh's Sanhani tribe were imposed in control over nearly all units, and corruption became endemic. One typical practice was for the officers to maintain their units at 70-80% of their nominal strength, collect pays and supplies as if their units were at 100% strength, while selling surplus arms and supplies on the black market. The situation reached such proportions that by 2010 nobody could say with any dose of certainty exactly how strong Yemen's regular armed forces were.[13]

Overhauling the Air Force

Under such conditions, the recovery of the Yemeni military after the Civil War of 1994 was relatively slow. Immediately after the war, the Yemen Air Force (YAF) spent months collecting and sorting out the extensive booty from the former PDRYAF. For all practical purposes, the resulting air force almost exclusively consisted of the former YARAF: although it occupied bases such as those in Aden, Anad and Riyan, and eventually inherited some of PDRYAF's personnel, its organizational structure and most unit designations remained those of the northern air force. Foremost, all major combat flying units were concentrated at bases like Daylami, Hudaydah, and the Tariq Hawban AB (military side of Ta'iz airport), while only Anad AB was retained in the south as a major training base.

In addition to bases, the YAF inherited a number of former South Yemeni aircraft. About a dozen each of MiG-21s and Su-22s were captured intact, as were several MiG-29s, a few Mi-25s, and a number of Mi-8s, Mi-17s, and Mi-14s. As soon as the process of sorting these out was completed, in 1996, the air force withdrew all the remaining Su-22s and Su-22Ms from service, and acquired four additional Su-17M-4Ks from Ukraine instead. The same country was then contracted to provide maintenance staff that helped overhaul about 20 Su-22M-3s and Su-22UM-3s in Yemen, and then to undertake similar work on 28 Su-22M-4Ks abroad. However, the process of overhauling Su-22s in Yemen came forward at such a slow pace, that in November 2005 Sana'a was forced to send 20 Su-22M-4Ks to Belarus, for overhauls at the 558th Aircraft Repair Plant.[14]

In 1999, the YAF decided to bolster its domestic training capabilities and acquired 12 Zlin Z-242 elementary trainers and 12 Aero L-39C Delfin jet trainers from the Czech Republic. These aircraft entered service with two units of the newly established Flight School based at Anad AB. For the first time in its history, the YAF thus took over the responsibility for providing basic training of all of its flying personnel. Another batch of 12 second hand but overhauled L-39Cs were acquired from Ukraine in 2005.

The backbone of the YAF's fighter fleet became MiG-29s. Impressed by the type it encountered in combat during the Civil War, Saleh's government not only acquired two additional examples from Kazakhstan, in 1995-1996, but in March 2000 opened negotiations with Moscow for the purchase of 24 upgraded examples. A contract for delivery of 14 MiG-29s and 1 MiG-29UB – and their upgrade and an upgrade of surviving examples obtained from other sources to SM standard – was signed a year later and deliveries took place between June 2002 and November 2004. Equipped with N019MP radar and an advanced fire-control system, Yemeni MiG-29s became the most advanced combat aircraft of the fleet. They were compatible with Kh-29T (ASCC code 'AS-14 Kedge') and Kh-31P ('AS-17 Krypton') guided air-to-surface missiles, and R-77 (Izdeliye-190) guided air-to-air missiles, small batches of which were purchased too. Six additional MiG-29SMs followed in 2004 and 2005, and it seems that by 2007 the fleet reached its peak strength of about 36 aircraft through additional deliveries.[15]

In 2003, Yemen opened negotiations with Singapore related to service-life-extension and an upgrade of surviving F-5s. However, no such deal ever materialized and the gradually diminishing fleet was maintained with the help of US aid packages instead. Searching for an alternative, in 2011, the YAF contracted the Ukrainian company Odesaviarem to overhaul 24 MiG-21bis' and 4 MiG-21UMs. Work on all aircraft was completed but the last 8 MiG-21s were never collected nor paid for by Yemen, and subsequently sold to Croatia instead.[16]

One of 12 L-39Cs Yemen purchased from the Czech Republic in 1999, as seen during a pre-delivery test flight. (Aero)

The first six MiG-29SMs delivered to Yemen in June 2002 were operated by No. 9 Squadron, YAF. Notable is the in-flight refuelling probe installed under the left side of the cockpit: since Yemen never operated any tanker aircraft, these were actually useless. (Pit Weinert Collection)

Some South Yemeni Su-22s were overhauled by foreign specialists in Yemen, usually at Daylami AB, as also was this Su-22M-3. (Pit Weinert Collection)

Air Defences and Ballistic Missiles

The condition of Yemen's ground-based air defences proved slightly more problematic. These were nominally integrated into the YAF and re-organized into a total of eight brigades, each of which operated a mix of SA-2, SA-3, SA-6 and SA-9 systems, and protected one of the major urban centres. Except for their own, integral sensors, there was no networking between these units: their

Locally-overhauled Su-22M-4s received a much lighter camouflage pattern than those overhauled in Ukraine in the late 2000s. This example – serial number 2227 – was photographed at Daylami AB in the late 2000s. (Pit Weinert Collection)

A row of Yemeni MiG-21bis' that were overhauled in Ukraine but never delivered back to Yemen. Notable is an entirely new camouflage pattern, similar to that applied on Su-22M-4 overhauled with Ukrainian support in Yemen. (Photo by Holger Müller)

command facilities, training, maintenance and overall readiness were poor, and electronic warfare capability virtually non-existent.

This began to change only in 2012 and 2013, when Sana'a contracted several Belarusian companies to overhaul and – partially – upgrade its ground-based air defences. Amongst others, most existing SA-3s were upgraded to the Pechora-2M standard. While the related work largely escaped public attention, it resulted in a situation where – due to combined effects of the work of foreign specialists, but also corruption and disorder within the air force (see next chapter) – ground-based air defences were in a better condition than flying units by 2014.[17]

Units equipped with ballistic missiles underwent a similar process. After the Civil War of 1994, they were consolidated within the 30,000-strong Republican Guard, meanwhile commanded by Saleh's son, Ahmed Ali Saleh. This included three units equipped with surface-to-surface missiles:

- 1st Artillery Brigade, equipped with 12 9K79 (ASCC-code SS-21 Scarab) systems, including 12 9M714 TELs and around 60 OTR-21 Tochka missiles;
- 26th Artillery Brigade, equipped with R-17/R-300 Elbrus (ASCC-code SS-1C Scud-B systems); and
- 89th Artillery Brigade, equipped with Luna-M (ASCC-code FROG-7) systems.

In 1999, Sana'a signed a contract with North Korea for the supply of 12 transporter-erector-launchers (TELs) for Hwasong-6 systems and an unknown quantity – probably around 80 – of associated missiles. Although shortly interrupted by the USA and its allies, their deliveries continued until 2002, by when Hwasong-6s replaced obsolete FROG-7s.[18]

A rare photograph of a Soviet-made RSP-7 or RSP-10 radar system (these two types are hard to distinguish even for professionals) used for ground-controlled approach. Although not related to air defence purposes, they are very important for every-day work of an air force like the YAF and remain in intensive use until today. A Ukrainian company overhauled and upgraded Yemeni RSP-7/10s in the mid-2000s. (Pit Weinert Collection)

Two of the SA-2 SAMs overhauled by Belarussian specialists in the late 2000s. (Pit Weinert Collection)

A rare photograph of two ZRK-BD Strela-1 (SA-9 Gaskin) armoured vehicles, as seen in Aden of the late 1980s. The unified Yemeni military inherited around two dozen of such air defence systems, equipped with four infra-red homing missiles each. (Pit Weinert Collection)

A 9P117M TEL with R-17E (SS-1C Scud-B) missile, as seen during a military parade in Sana'a of the late 1990s. (Pit Weinert Collection)

New Horizons

During the 1990s two new threats for the central government in Sana'a emerged: one in the form of the so-called Houthis; the other in form of what eventually transformed into the organization known as the 'al-Qaeda in the Arabian Peninsula' (AQAP). Relations between these two groups, Saleh's government, but also multiple foreign powers were to prove decisive for the history of Yemen ever since.

The core of Shafi Islamists in Yemen is centred around the once-powerful al-Fadhli tribe. Based in the Abyan Province, the Fadhli lost their lands to the Marxists in former South Yemen of the 1980s, and then found themselves sidelined even further after the Civil War of 1994. Nevertheless, the Fadhli began receiving some support from private sources in Saudi Arabia. When hundreds of young Yemenis – some of these with direct connections to Osama Bin Laden – returned from the 'holy war' (Jihad) in Afghanistan, most of these gathered around this tribe. In the early 1990s, the Jihadists established their first camp in Sa'ada Province, near the Saudi border, which turned into a gathering point for ever more of Wahhabists from Egypt, Jordan, Saudi Arabia, Syria and elsewhere. Facing their – gradually intensifying – campaign of attacks on Western tourists, in 1994 Saleh brokered a deal with the Fadhil: their leader was released from jail in return for providing support during the Civil War of 1994.

After that conflict, Fadhil had his sister marry Brigadier-General Ali Mohsen al-Ahmar, then still Saleh's close friend and the commander of the 1st Armoured Division, but already renowned for heavily Islamist leanings. In similar fashion, other members of the growing group were rewarded for their loyalty to Saleh with positions throughout the Yemeni security and intelligence apparatus: indeed, they de-facto took over the Political Security Organization (PSO; about 150,000 strong) once this was separated from the Ministry of Interior and became responsible directly to the president. Together with Mohsen, they played a crucial role in protecting Saleh from several coup attempts.

Around the same time the Wahhabists around Fadhil began their climb to power, circles within Saudi Arabia also began supporting the creation of the Islamic Front – a Muslim Brotherhood-affiliated militia that came into being in 1990. Following the unification of Yemen this was re-organized as the Islah Party, and became a coalition of tribal and religious elements that launched a campaign of spreading Wahhabism in Yemen.

The third group of Shafi Islamists that crystallized between the 1990s and 2000s are variously called 'Quietists' or 'Dammaj Salafis' in Yemen. Founded by Sheikh Muqbil Ibn Haid al-Wadi in the 1980s, this network became affiliated with the Dar al-Hadith network of tribes that established its 'headquarters' – including the central madrassa (religious school) – in Dammaj. While often misidentified as Wahhabists by foreign observers, the ideology of the groups is based on that of Shafi reformists from the 18th Century. Initially existing in some sort of agreement with Wahhabists, the Quietists gradually distanced themselves from Wahhabism and began emphasising their Yemeni character, as well as pointing out that their resistance against the Saudis and Wahhabism can be traced back to the 1920s.

Fearful of a possible US attack following 9/11, but also of all the power he provided to them, Saleh subsequently devised a strategy of gradually marginalizing the Wahhabists and other Islamists. As so often in similar situations, he did so foremost through the reorganization of his military. As well as appointing his son Ahmed Ali as the head of the Republican Guard and commander of Special Operation Forces, he put his nephews – Yahya Mohammed and Tariq, sons of his brother Muhammad Abdullah Saleh – the Chief of Staff of Central Security Forces and the US-funded Counter-Terrorism Unit (CSF & CTU, about 50,000 strong), and the Special Guard (counter-terrorist unit of the Republican Guard), respectively. These units and the National Security Bureau – created with US help in 2002 – received most of the US financial aid provided to Yemen during the 2000s.

A long row of YAF Su-22s parked on the central apron of Daylami AB. Although older than MiG-29SMs, and including an exotic mix of Su-17M-4s, Su-22M-3s, Su-22M-4s, and Su-22UM-3s, this type formed the backbone of the Yemeni air force in the 2000s. (Pit Weinert Collection)

Meanwhile, Saleh sacked one after another of Ali Mohsen's allies and, in order to further weaken their influence, ordered the headquarters of the 1st Armoured Division to be re-located from Sana'a to Amran, while most of the heavy equipment of this unit was re-assigned to the Republican Guard. Although thus distanced from the centres of power in Yemen, and weakened in terms of firepower, Mohsen, the Islah Party and various Wahhabist and Salafist groups could still easily put up to 100,000 men under arms. Nominally, they remained loyal to Saleh, nevertheless.

The Houthis

Instead of openly turning against Ali Mohsen and various Saudi-supported Islamists, during the 2000s, Saleh sought to use these groups for a war against another new emergence: the so-called Houthis.

The original impetus for the build-up of this movement was provided by several developments, including an expulsion of more than one million Yemeni guest-workers from Saudi Arabia in 1990, and the return of thousands of others from different states of the Gulf Cooperation Council, but also from Saleh's victory in the Civil War of 1994. The returnees found their homeland dominated by Saleh and his family, and a clique of related or befriended top military commanders and merchants – all tied to the Saudi-run patronage networks – that amassed immense wealth at the expense of nearly everybody else. Around the same time the first post-Imamate generation of Zaidis reached maturity. A combination of increased literacy and the exposure to the outside world resulted in their increasing material expectations, and a disappointment with existing political structures. Confronted with the Saudi-supported spread of Salafism and Wahhabism, many young Zaidis excelled in religious learning – which in turn enabled them to challenge the traditional elites. This mix resulted in a period known as 'Zaidi revival', during which the Houthis – named after the family of their first leader, Hussayn al-Houthi, who studied religion in Sudan – emerged as the strongest new political movement.[19]

Far from being supported by all the Zaidis, or anything like 'Iranian proxies', as often explained by their opponents, the Houthis found themselves in confrontation not only with representatives of much of the Hashd tribal confederation, but with government officials too.[20] With Saleh ignoring their demands, a direct confrontation became inevitable – even more so because the area from which most original Houthis came is renowned as one where arms trafficking is as normal, and as important, for the local economy as exporting livestock and wheat to Saudi Arabia, or grapes, raisins, pomegranates, coffee and sandstones to Sana'a. The appearance of armed Houthis alarmed Saleh: fearing a possible uprising and forced into action by demands from the Shafi Islamist block, he began issuing fiery accusations. When these showed no effect, he ordered an arrest of Hussein al-Houthi, and launched a violent crackdown on his organization.

Military Organization of the Houthis

As of 2004, and for most of the following six years, the Houthis had no clearly determined political and military organization:

their command, recruiting, and combat structures emerged over time on the basis of personal relations. Their command structure during this period was centred on Badr ad-Din al-Houthi, Hussayn al-Houthi, Yahya al-Houthi, and Abdullah ar-Razzami, who variously served as spokespersons for the group at home or abroad, as its ideologists, or as political leaders. Another important person emerged in the form of Salih Habra: this harsh critic of the Saleh government also served as a spokesperson for the Houthi group, and subsequently became involved in negotiating with Sana'a.[21]

Eventually, top military commanders became those persons that also established and maintained a sense of group ideology: Hussayn al-Houthi served as the movement's military commander during the first phase of the subsequent war, Badr ad-Din took over during the second, and Abd al-Malik during the third phase. Therefore, the title of 'military commander' of Houthis during the first phases of their conflict can only be described as 'nominal': rugged terrain and poor means of communication usually meant that the actual reach of top commanders was limited to their immediate surroundings, and many of them operated in isolation from each other. For example, Hussayn initially commanded groups in the Marran mountains, Badr ad-Din in the Nushr and an-Naqa area, while Abd al-Malik operated out of an-Naqa and Matra. Unsurprisingly, some foreign observers introduced the 'rank' of 'local area leader' (LAL) to designate them, instead. Many LALs assumed aliases, while others became famous after their tribal names, which not only made their identification a particularly problematic issue, but indicated the heterogenous nature of the organization, different parts of which have had different aims, too.

The primary combat formations of the Houthis were units ranging in size from squads to platoons. Initially, most of these operated on direct orders from top commanders. As the movement grew, a second level of leadership developed – initially occupied by relatives or close friends. Due to frequent targeting of their headquarters, Houthi commanders learned to often change their bases. Indeed, although maintaining their authority, with time top Houthi leaders became ever more distanced from the planning and execution of every-day combat operations. Instead, they became dependent on the cultivation of loyalty through influence and persuasion – instead intimidation and authoritarian control. In turn, the LALs obtained ever more autonomy: by 2009, they became entirely free to plan, initiate or end engagements at their own discretion, thus largely neutralising the government's attempts to target specific leaders.

This development of decentralized leadership greatly influenced the way the Houthis sustained themselves materially.

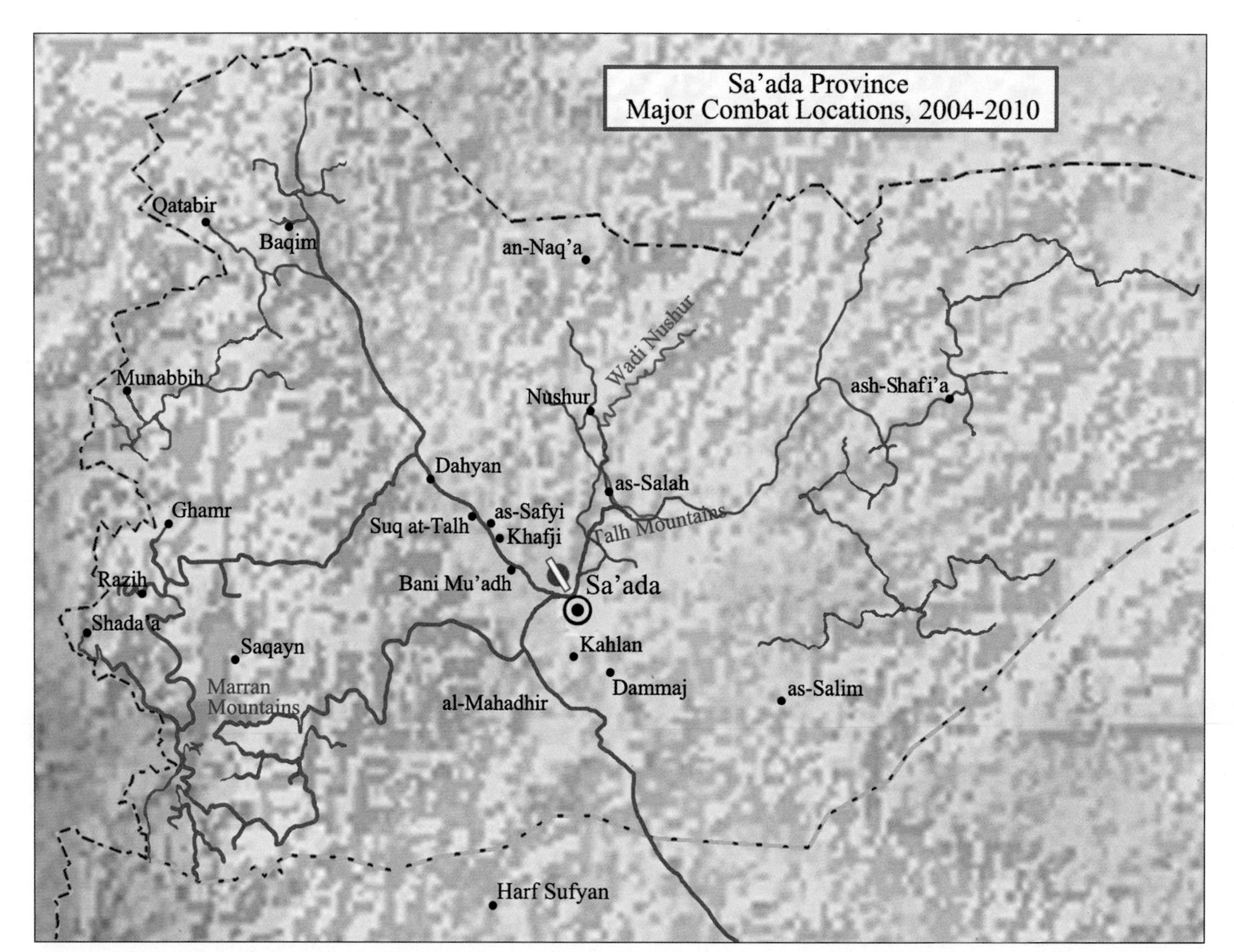

Map 1 Principal combat locations from the six Sa'ada Wars, fought 2004-2010. Notable is that most of the fighting was concentrated on the western side of the Sa'ada province, along the Saudi border, roughly in the area between Qatarib in the north and Marran Mountains in the south. It is also in this mountainous area that most of the population of this province live – usually in villages with fewer than 500 inhabitants. (Map by Tom Cooper)

Residents of Sa'ada survived in near-complete isolation from the outside world since earlier times, and the manhood in this part of Yemen in particular was associated with the possession of weapons. There were estimates about Yemeni tribes holding a stock of up to 5 million small arms as of the early 2000s.[22] Such widespread availability of arms eliminated the need for an organized procurement and distribution of the same. Something similar can be said about the issue of acquisition and distribution of food, clothes, and means of transportation. Indeed, quite early during their insurgency, the Houthis even began fashioning their own sniper rifles.

The issue of sources of arms for Houthis became ever more important the more the government in Sana'a – followed by the Saudi government, and then various Israeli and US think-tanks – accused the insurgents of operating outside the Yemeni social system, and then of being Iranian proxies. In response, the Houthis persistently highlighted their Yemeni origins and allegiance to the Yemeni constitution, and that they were abiding by traditions of autonomy in northern Yemen. They openly distanced themselves from Iran, too: when asked about possible connections to Tehran Abd al-Malik once claimed, 'the government surely knows that it is a false and fake claim that does not contain any evidence'. Furthermore, he stressed that the Houthis need not obtain weapons abroad because, '…the Yemeni people are armed people… arms markets are scattered across numerous governorates'.[23]

Certainly enough, the longer the war between Sana'a and the Houthis lasted, the more arms were captured by the Houthis from the Yemeni Army. In 2009 in particular, the insurgency overran several sizeable depots of the Yemeni Army and disarmed numerous units. It was in this fashion that the insurgents obtained not only large stocks of machine guns (MGs) and rocket-propelled grenades (RPGs), but also man-portable air defence systems (MANPADs, also 'shoulder launched surface to air missiles'). Furthermore, they captured increasing numbers of military vehicles, including armoured personnel carriers (APCs), and a few main battle tanks (MBTs). Any 'extras' were obtained from arms dealers and through the means of smuggling. Sources outside Sa'ada became important only during the late 2000s, when the Houthis began acquiring cellular and satellite telephones, and using these for communication purposes.

To a certain degree, the Houthi military tactics during the first few years of the movement were at least roughly comparable to that of many other insurgencies previously run in areas dominated by rugged terrain. Initial operations consisted of hit-and-run attacks on minor military and police bases and checkpoints. During the next phase of the conflict, military officials and convoys became a primary target: initially for attacks with small arms fire, then for attacks with heavier armament – like Soviet-made ZU-23 anti-aircraft guns and various mortars in the 60-81mm calibre range, and then by the means of improvised explosive devices (IEDs). By 2005, the Houthis established a number of their own checkpoints thus curtailing military movement – but also the transport of civilians sympathetic to the government – in large parts of the Sa'ada province. A year later, they began launching commando-style operations against selected targets inside urban areas, and then running entire campaigns of demolishing roads, bridges and electricity stations, effectively cutting off all the roads south of Sa'ada. Beginning in 2007 and 2008, the Houthis began combining different, autonomous groups of their combatants to carry out complex offensive operations. However, it was only years later that the insurgents established something similar to a 'standing army', with at least two battalion-sized units.

First Five Sa'ada Wars

On 18 June 2004, a column of the 310th Armoured Brigade of the Yemeni Army, commanded by Brigadier-General Qushaibi, drove into the Marran area of Haydan District, provoking a battle with the Houthis that lasted nearly three and a half months. Early during this campaign, the Yemeni military and security forces primarily operated from garrisons in Sa'ada (Akwan), Suq at-Talh and Walad Masoud, in addition to some border posts near Saudi Arabia, all of which were constructed since 2002.

Operating a modern military in the Sa'ada area remains nearly impossible to this day – at least without air support. The mountainous terrain impedes not only the manoeuvrability of any kind of vehicles, but even of the infantry. On the other side, the geography of this part of Yemen creates networks and the means for the locals to endure conflict over long periods of time, and exploit the situation to their advantage. The very limited number of roads and mountain tracks renders these exposed to mines and ambushes, while the knowledge of the most essential locations – such as sources of water and food – is reserved for the locals. Therefore, the YAF was to play an important, even if badly underreported role in the following conflict. This role was further limited by the levels to which Saleh actually wanted to support the operations in question. The majority of units deployed to fight the Houthis belonged to parts of the military controlled by Major-General Ali Mohsen al-Ahmar. Saleh was seeking at least as much to destroy Houthis as for these to cause attrition to the units controlled by Ahmar, but also to tarnish the reputation of that general. Therefore, he often curbed support provided by the YAF, especially when Ali Mohsen's forces appeared to be on the verge of a major victory. Nevertheless, supported by YAF Mi-8/17 and Mi-25 helicopters, the 310th Armoured Brigade continued raiding the Sa'ada governorate until they killed Hussayn al-Houthi, sometime in September 2004.

Hussayn's brother Badr ad-Din al-Houthi took over and travelled to Sana'a in an attempt to negotiate with Saleh: the Yemeni president ignored him. As soon as Badr ad-Din returned to Sa'ada, in March 2005, government officials accused the Houthis of attempting to buy more arms and fighting broke out in al-Khafji. In December 2005, another firefight erupted in Suq at-Talh.

In January 2006, YAF helicopters deployed commandos along the roads and tracks in the direction of ash-Shafia, Wadi Nushur and ar-Razzamat. The 101st, 103rd, and the 115th Brigades then followed on the ground. The Houthis resisted, and several bitter battles developed, the insurgents losing two of their top commanders in Wadi Nushur area. Although this operation failed to reach any of its actual objectives, Saleh then announced the end of combat operations, and an amnesty for insurgents, on 16 April 2005. However, the fighting went on, with Houthis continuing to ambush army columns and attack military outposts: no matter how limited in scope, the government's decision to deploy a military force into autonomous tribal areas, where mediation – even if including violent rhetoric – traditionally served as the means to pre-empt violence, and Saleh's refusals to negotiate with the Houthis, represented a major violation of local cultural norms. Such behaviour ruined the reputation of the Yemeni president and drove additional youngsters into the arms of the insurgency.

As the unrest continued spreading, in late December 2005 the Houthis launched their first offensive and captured al-Khafji. The YAF reacted with air strikes on as-Salim, as-Syfi, Talh, and Bani Mua'adh, but these left no lasting impressions upon insurgents. By the end of the month, they were already at the entrance to Sa'ada, where the 115th Brigade entrenched. An entire series of ambushes, attacks and assassinations of government officials and rival tribal chiefs followed, in reaction to which Saleh ordered the next military campaign.

This was opened in January 2006 by YAF air strikes on all known and suspected Houthi positions. Bani Mu'adh, Talh, as-Sayfi, al-Khafji, al-Amar, Wadi Nushur, Hamazat, and al-Naq'a were repeatedly bombed by F-5Es, MiG-21s and Su-22s. Lasting at least a week, this effort paved the way for an advance of six army brigades supported by tanks and heavy artillery. The Houthis reacted with countless ambushes, but also blew up one of the bridges on the road connecting Sa'ada with Sana'a, before re-deploying most of their forces into the area between Razih and Dahyan, from where they counterattacked and surrounded an army brigade in Maran, in March 2006. Unnerved, the government reacted by unleashing the YAF into a series of particularly devastating air strikes, but most of these hit the local population instead of insurgents.

In mid-March 2006, the Army launched its next campaign by advancing on Dahyan, a town on the only road to a number of Houthi strongholds in the northwest of the Sa'ada governorate. The YAF heavily bombed this town, destroying much of the infrastructure and religious sites, however, the two Army brigades involved were repeatedly ambushed and finally mauled while attempting to assault the place. As all efforts to dislodge the insurgents failed, the number of air strikes increased. In an attempt to lessen the burden on its pilots and ground personnel, the YAF then attempted forward-deploying its fighter-bombers at Sa'ada airfield. This practice was discontinued after two MiG-29s collided and crashed while landing in shear-wind, on 7 March that year, killing one of the pilots.[24]

Through early 2007, the Houthis continued increasing pressure upon army units in the Bani M'adh and Dahyan districts. By 4 April 2007, Army units surrounding Dahyan were forced to withdraw from most of their positions. The following night, several platoon-sized Houthi groups launched coordinated attacks on outposts in the al-Ghabir region and overran most of these, capturing a significant amount of arms and ammunition – including mortars. On 5 April, the Daris tribe – which sided with Sana'a – attempted to counterattack but additional Houthi groups cut off all the roads through Wadi Badir and Ghamr districts, preventing the arrival of army reinforcements: indeed, an entire convoy approaching the Dahyan area was destroyed in an ambush. When Sana'a reacted by deploying at least a battalion of the Republican Guards, supported by helicopters, the Houthis quickly evaded by withdrawing and disappearing into the mountains. Overall, in a matter of only three days, the insurgents hit nearly all government positions in central Sa'ada, clearly demonstrating their ability to run coordinated operations, interrupt logistics and assault tribes allied with Sana'a, too. Although suffering higher casualties than the government, their attacks sapped the morale and strength of the army and allied forces, preventing government forces from reaching any of their objectives, and having one of the Army's brigades trapped in the mountains of Maran – where its troops were able to survive only thanks to supplies flown in by YAF helicopters. Foremost, the Houthi leadership survived and presented itself victorious even in battles fought in urban areas. Taken aback by this setback, Saleh's government was rather relieved to accept a Qatar-brokered peace deal that ended this phase of fighting in February 2008.

Considering THE uncompromising positions of all involved parties, it was unsurprising that the related deal never materialised. When the Houthis refused to disarm, the Army launched an attempt to lift the siege of the brigade in Maran. Usually described as the fifth campaign – or the 'Fifth Sa'ada War' – this operation began with days-long air strikes flown by YAF fighter-bombers and helicopters, but ended without success and quite suddenly, on 16 July 2008, when Saleh once again declared the conflict with the Houthis to be over. Not entirely satisfied with their situation, the Houthis continued to fight and by early August not only captured most of Sa'ada governorate, but neutralised most of the government's local support base, too.[25]

A still from a video showing the wreckage of the YAF Mi-171Sh that crashed in rugged terrain of the Sa'aba governorate on 3 December 2007. (Pit Weinert Collection)

A still from a video showing the wreckage of one of two MiG-29s that collided during landing at Sa'ada airfield on 7 March 2007. (Pit Weinert Collection)

YAF helicopters – like this Mi-171Sh – played a very important role during early campaigns against the Houthis. They were deployed not only for assault purposes and in bombing attacks, but foremost to transport commandos, reinforcements, and supplies. (Pit Weinert Collection)

Operation Scorched Earth

After a period of reorganizing and resupplying, Major-General Ali Mohsen concentrated about 30,000 troops for a new, sixth offensive on Sa'ada, in July 2009. Code-named Operation Scorched Earth, this was supported by a significant portion of militias from the Hashd tribal confederation, but also two brigades from the Republican Guards, and the YAF.

Operation Scorched Earth began on 11 August 2009 with air strikes against all known arms depots and petroleum storage areas. Seeking to hit the Houthi supply convoys, assault helicopters of the Yemeni Air Force targeted road traffic in the Sa'ada governorate but also up to Harf Sofiyan district of Amran governorate (about 140 kilometres north of Sa'ada). Dozens of vehicles and over 100 insurgents (including two of their commanders) and civilians were killed.[26] On 29 August 2009, multiple formations of YAF fighter-bombers bombed Saqin, Yasnam, Sudan, al-Ind and Maran, killing another insurgent commander. The Houthis reacted by staging their first 'large' operation: in mid-September 2017, they concentrated several dozens of their squads and platoons to launch a well-coordinated, multi-prong assault on the Presidential Palace in Sa'ada city. Reportedly supported by 'more than 60 armoured vehicles', this attack appears to have mauled the 115th Brigade: this lost up to 70 of its vehicles and dozens of troops killed. While the government subsequently claimed to have thwarted this attack and killed 140 killed insurgents, even its own reports made it clear that this assault went on for days and prompted the YAF to deploy its helicopters in support of ground troops. Elsewhere, a Houthi counteroffensive was successful in securing Munabbih, on the border to Saudi Arabia, to which the YAF reacted with a – meanwhile usual – campaign of air strikes. Reportedly, alone the first of these killed more than 80 civilians on 16 September 2009.[27]

As the fighting grew in intensity, the YAF began suffering losses. The first of these occurred on 2 October 2009, when a MiG-21 was claimed shot down by Houthi ground fire over Marazen. By 5 December, Houthis claimed no less than four YAF fighter-bombers as shot down, mostly in the Sa'ada area (for known details on YAF's attrition between 2001 and 2014, see Table 1). Curiously, while officials in Sana'a explained most of these as technical malfunctions, the Western media began publishing reports about Iran supplying the Houthis with Chinese-made QW-1M or Iranian-made Misagh-1 MANPADs. However, evidence for deliveries of any kind of arms of Iranian origin was never provided. On the contrary, available visual evidence, communications between Sana'a, various foreign intelligence agencies, and the US State Department have all repeatedly shown that whatever air defence weapons were operated by the Houthis – all were either captured on the battlefield, or acquired from local arms merchants, just not from Iran.[28]

Unsurprisingly considering rapid growth of the Houthi military prowess, and the general condition of the Yemeni state and its military, by late October 2009, nearly all forces commanded by Major-General Ali Mohsen al-Ahmar in Sa'ada and Amran governorates were in serious trouble. One of six brigades involved was overrun by insurgents, two others besieged, and the Houthis captured the town of Razih, together with the nearby airfield and two military bases including sizeable stocks of arms, ammunition and supplies. The YAF bombed all three locations intensively on 23 and 24 October, apparently in an attempt to destroy some of the equipment left behind, but such efforts proved to be the literal 'drop in the bucket'.[29]

A pair of YAF Sukhois seen underway near Sana'a in the mid-2000s. The aircraft in the front is a two-seat Su-22UM-3, the one to the rear belongs to a batch of 20 Su-22M-4s overhauled in Ukraine. (Pit Weinert Collection)

YAF helicopters – like this Mi-8 – flew intensive operations during most of the six Sa'ada Wars, providing fire-support and delivering crucial supplies to army units cut off by insurgents. (Albert Grandolini Collection)

Saudi Intervention

On 1 November 2009, the Houthis accused the government of Saudi Arabia of allowing Yemeni Army units to make use of Saudi territory. Correspondingly, the insurgents crossed the border and occupied Jebel Dukhan and two other dominating peaks nearby, where they clashed with elements of the Royal Saudi armed forces for the first time.

While neither side ever published a detailed account of what exactly happened during these first clashes, the picture that can be reconstructed on the basis of dozens of different reports is that the Houthis attacked two camps of the Royal Saudi Border Guard, prompting the Royal Saudi Land Forces (RSLF) to hit back. Deploying elements of the 33rd Infantry Battalion RSLF and the 2nd Marine Battalion of the Royal Saudi Naval Forces (RSNF) into counterattacks on well-concealed positions in a rush and – apparently – expecting the Houthis to run at their sight, the Saudis were repeatedly ambushed and suffered heavy losses. Even close air support operations by Boeing F-15S fighter-bombers of Khamis Mushayt-based Nos 6 and 55 Squadrons, RSAF could not change the situation: on the contrary, several of these returned to their base with bullet holes from ground fire.

Stunned with this experience, the Saudis stopped and entrenched, while bringing in reinforcements and reorganizing their forces to operate in a more methodical fashion. Elements of the 1st, 10th, and 14th Brigades of the RSLF, and the 18th Brigade of the RSNF were ordered into the area, together with the 85th Commando Battalion, which was airlifted to the battlefield. Interviewed on condition of anonymity, a retired RSAF F-15 pilot described what happened next:

> After the rush of the first two days of the conflict, when the first forces arrived and we suffered most of the casualties of that war – primarily due to the lack of intelligence and well-dug-in insurgents being in control of the high ground – the conflict was handled in a very professional manner. A joint headquarters was established for all of the involved forces, including commanders of our infantry, armour, artillery, air force, special forces etc.... This had an Air Support Operations Centre (ASOC) assigned, where basically all of the aerial operations were planned.... On the third day of the war, the RSAF was ordered to fly at higher altitude in order to avoid the ground fire. There was no longer any need to fly at low level upon arrival of our joint tactical air controllers, equipped with unmanned aerial vehicles (UAVs), as well as six AH-64 Apache attack helicopters. RSAF pilots did occasionally use flares afterwards, because there was no certainty if the enemy was equipped with shoulder-fired missiles or not.[30]

Emboldened by their defensive success, the Houthis attempted to advance on Najran, on 4 or 5 November, but their convoy was destroyed by RSAF fighter-bombers well before reaching its target. By 7 November, Tornado IDS' from Dhahran/King Abdul Aziz AB-based Nos 75 and 83 Squadrons became involved too:

> It got pretty busy down there, and so to take some pressure off the F-15s, Tornados flew air strikes from Dhahran, refuelling from tankers in the air. During the second week of the war, a detachment of 18 Tornados was re-deployed to Khamis Mushayt.

A combination of sustained air strikes and artillery barrages forced the surviving Houthis to withdraw from Jebel Dukhan on 5-6 November, but those at Jebel ar-Ramih and Jebel Dawd held their positions and fought back fiercely. In order to isolate them, the RSAF began striking selected targets inside Yemen, including Malaheez, Hassameh and Shida.[31] Another retired officer of the Royal Saudi armed forces explained:

> 'Our intelligence estimated the Houthi fighting force at about 50,000 of battle-hardened, ideologically driven, well organized, well funded fighters, trained by Hezbollah from Lebanon and the Iranian Revolutionary Guards Corps. Our intelligence further indicated that Houthis had six years of combat experience and were de-facto winning against Yemeni government before they attacked Saudi Arabia.'[32]

Through mid and late November 2009, the RSAF continued pounding the Houthis at Ramih and Dawd while the Saudi ground forces prepared their next assault. Most of the fighting took place in mountainous terrain, in the rare air high above the sea surface. Since not all of the Saudi forces involved were mountain-trained, some needed time to acclimatise to the local circumstances. A retired RSAF F-15-pilot described how the Saudi air force organized its close-air-support operations:

> At the beginning of the conflict, up to 75% of RSAF's missions – and these reached more than 40 sorties a day at one point – were flown for CAS purposes. Over the time, that percentage changed as the situation on the ground changed. Later during the war, only about 10% of our sorties resulted in provision of close air support...The method of organizing such operations was to always have at least two aircraft airborne in holding patterns within 10 minutes flying time from the combat zone, and two others on alert on the ground. This was in addition to other aircraft with specialized purposes.... There were no more maintenance issues than during routine, peace-time operations. The crews flying combat sorties were the same flying peace-time sorties, they trained for this for years. Furthermore, we always had standby aircraft on the ground, ready to execute specific kinds of missions, plus spares ready to take the place of those that had to abort...In two months of most intensive operations, we only witnessed two ground aborts by F-15s. One had a problem with a radio, don't know what the other had. During the same period of time, there were seven ground aborts by Tornados. Both figures were consistent with the numbers we usually see during peace-time operations. Our Tornados always had a higher rate of ground aborts than F-15s – one similar to that of Tornados operated by the RAF or the German Luftwaffe, but slightly better than that of the Italian air force.

The short war between the Houthis and Saudi Arabia was the baptism of fire for the custom-tailored F-15S variant of the powerful Strike Eagle multi-role fighter. This photograph shows an example from No. 55 Squadron, which played a very important role in the course of this conflict. (via Tom Cooper)

A Panavia Tornado IDS (most Saudi examples were meanwhile upgraded to the GR.Mk 4 standard) from No. 66 Squadron RSAF seen preparing for a training flight in the early 1990s. Notable is the Damocles targeting pod installed under the fuselage. (Photo by Jean-Marie Lipka)

An AH-64A of the RSLF circling a forward operations site before landing after a combat sortie against the Houthis. As far as is known, the RSLF was still working-up its force of more than 70 Apaches at the time of the first conflict between the Houthis and Saudi Arabia. Because of this, only six these attack helicopters got involved. The Houthis claimed one of them shot down, but none was actually lost. (M. T. L. Collection)

Two Houthi combatants with the empty shell of a US-made cluster bomb deployed by the RSAF over Northern Yemen in 2009. (M. T. L.)

Naval Blockade

On 29 October 2009, Sana'a claimed that its naval forces had stopped an Iranian vessel carrying a shipment of arms for insurgents. However, it transpired that the ship in question – *Mahan-1* – was underway in ballast to the Iranian port of Bandar Anzali, on the Azov Sea. Unsurprisingly, all the related reporting stopped once the ship was found empty. Nevertheless, Saudi Arabia then imposed a naval blockade of the Red Sea coast of Yemen on 10 November. By that time, the aviation of the Royal Saudi Navy (RSNF) – including Aerospatiale/Eurocopter AS.332 Super Puma armed helicopters – became involved, although it seems that most of the time this happened rather by accident than by design, as explained by another retired Saudi officer:

> The RSNF aviation was used foremost to fly resupply missions for Marines and Navy Special Forces. They did use their guns and unguided rockets to provide some support on several occasions, but did not really fly close air support. That was the job of Army's AH-64s...Nevertheless, our Navy did intercept and sink a number of ships carrying arms and supplies from Eritrea and Somalia.

In addition to interdicting naval traffic, through November, the Saudis continued interdicting Houthi supply links inside Yemen. Tornados and F-15S' from Khamis Mushayt flew 28 combat sorties on the morning of 13 November 2009 alone, while the YAF added to the pressure by heavily bombing Bani Maan – one of the best-fortified Houthi strongholds – on 14 November. Sa'ada, where a Yemeni commando brigade was meanwhile besieged by the insurgents, was heavily bombed on 16 November, when up to 120 were killed, including many civilians.

Having prepared the battlefield and softened enemy positions, the Saudi ground forces assaulted Jebel Ramih and Jebel Dawd on 18 November 2009. The Houthis claimed to have recovered both peaks and caused heavy casualties two days later. However, there is little doubt that they were overwhelmed by massive volumes of artillery fire and air strikes, had suffered heavy losses, and were forced to withdraw. Indeed, two days later the RSLF even launched a limited advance several kilometres deep into Yemen, in the direction of the town of Razah.[33]

With ground forces firmly in control, the RSAF returned to flying interdiction strikes. Saqayn was bombed on 27 November and al-Ammar on 30 November, prompting Houthis to complain bitterly about massive civilian casualties. The government in Riyadh denied any related allegations, while former RSAF-pilots explained:

> We extensively, throughout the entire conflict, deployed special forces that operated UAVs with night capability to monitor insurgent activity inside Yemen. They often called for air strikes on targets of opportunity...Our military intelligence and electronic warfare units picked up communications in Farsi on numerous occasions. They also identified a camp where Hezbollah were training Houthis – and this was then destroyed by the RSAF. After-action reports indicated nearly everybody there was killed by that air strike: our intelligence intercepted radio messages in which insurgents were accusing each other of being Saudi agents because of the precision of our attack.

On 15 December 2009, RSAF involvement in this war reached its peak with about 70 combat sorties flown against such insurgent strongholds as al-Jaberi, Shatha and Jaza', Dhohian, Tokya, Yasnam and Ashash. The Saudis continued their campaign until 22 December, when Riyadh announced the 'bulk of operations against Houthis' as over and confirmed a loss of 73 killed and 30 missing in action.

Undeterred, the insurgents continued fighting, provoking further air strikes. Raqqa, Sabbah and Malaheet were hit on the same day, and dozens of other towns and villages during the following weeks. On 7 January 2010, the YAF bombed Farwa and the Sa'ada area in an attempt to lessen the Houthi pressure on one of the besieged army brigades, but the insurgents then captured all three military bases in this part of the governorate. According to a retired Saudi F-15 pilot, this was not the least surprising:

> We attempted to share intelligence with Yemeni Military Intelligence, but they failed to make use of it. For example, we provided a list of all radio frequencies used by the Houthis, but Yemeni military intelligence neither listened to the Houthi radio traffic, nor attempted to jam it...Their cooperation with local tribes was non-existent... Our impression was that the Houthis penetrated the Yemeni military.

Rather gradually, the Saudis came to the conclusion that they were not fighting the same war as Saleh's government, as described by the same source:

> Yemeni intelligence provided coordinates for our air force to bomb and we launched the mission. But once over the target our pilots sensed that something was wrong and requested to be recalled back to base. Back on the ground, we cross-examined their data with that provided by the Yemenis and realized that Saleh gave us the coordinates of Major-General Ali Mohsen's headquarters. He wanted us to kill him. It was a very important lesson for us.

By mid-January, Abd al-Malik al-Houthi, the new leader of the insurgency, began making overtures for withdrawals from the Saudi border on condition of the Saudis stopping their bombing. However, the RSAF kept up the pressure. In about 20 airstrikes flown by Saudi F-15S' on 19 January 2010, even Abd al-Malik was seriously injured. Additional operations resulted in bombing of Houthi positions at Jebel al-Madood, Qafarah, al-Majdaha, Qamamat, Malaheet, al-Minzala and al-Jibiri, on 24 January, confirming that the Saudi effort was meanwhile focused on lessening the insurgent pressure upon the Yemeni military. Although effects of Saudi airstrikes were grossly downplayed by the insurgents – or declared as intentionally targeting civilians – they did deliver severe blows and forced the Houthis to accept all of the Government's and Saudi conditions on 25 January 2010. A cease-fire was in force on 11 February 2010 and two weeks later the Houthis withdrew their forces even from Sa'ada, thus enabling locals to return and start rebuilding the town.[34]

Overall, Operation Scorched Earth ended in an unmitigated disaster for the Yemeni government and its military. It left the

Houthis in control over most of Sa'ada, all of Amran, most of Jawf, and all of Hajjah governorates. Only the strategic mistake of attacking Saudi Arabia exposed the Houthis to the firepower of an opponent they could not defeat. On the contrary, the Saudi fire-power and mobility not only caused them heavy losses, but made it increasingly harder for the Houthis to manoeuvre around the battlefield – and thus contributed significantly to the insurgent decision to accept a cease-fire.

A gun-pod armed AS.332 Super Puma of the RSNF taking off from a forward base where also two AH-64 Apache helicopters were deployed. Saudi Super Pumas were primarily deployed for maritime patrol over the Red Sea and for distributing supplies to Saudi Marines, but they did get involved into several fire-fights with the Houthis too. (via Tom Cooper)

Most of the nine brigades of the Yemen Army deployed in the Sa'ada Province during the Sixth Sa'ada War suffered extensive losses in the course of the campaigns of 2009-2010. This still from a video shows a T-55 main battle tank, captured by Houthi insurgents. (Houthi release)

Houthi insurgents atop a badly damaged BRDM-2 armoured scout car, captured during the fighting in late 2009. (Pit Weinert Collection)

CHAPTER 3
BEGINNING OF THE END

Parallel with the flood of reports about intensive battles all over north-western Yemen, about the collapse of some of the involved Yemen Army's units and mass desertions of others, in mid-November 2009, reports began to surface about a new kind of conflict in Yemen. Correspondingly, a number of villages in Abyan province were bombed and up to 70 people – foremost civilians – were killed. Over the following weeks, it transpired that at least a few of the attacks in question were undertaken by US forces, which targeted terrorists of AQAP.

Originally led by Yemeni national Nasser al-Wuhayshi, and established through the merger of the al-Qaeda groups from Saudi Arabia and from Yemen in 2009, AQAP developed into what Washington eventually declared as 'the most dangerous branches of the terrorist network'. The US military began running covert operations against related groups in Yemen following the bombing of *USS Cole* (DDG-67), while this guided missile destroyer was refuelled in the port of Aden, on 12 October 2000. For most of the following eight years, operations against AQAP in Yemen were undertaken in the form of sporadic air strikes by so-called 'unmanned aerial vehicles' (UAVs).

During the period 2004-2009, Saleh avoided a direct confrontation with the predecessors of AQAP. However, as the Yemeni military became preoccupied with fighting the Houthis, and private interests in Saudi Arabia and Qatar began sponsoring AQAP as a new counterweight to the Houthis and President Saleh – widely considered 'apostates' and 'disloyal' in both countries, respectively – a sort of security vacuum developed elsewhere in Yemen, enabling the Jihadists to increase their activities. Obviously, this was against US interests. While completely ignoring Saudi involvement, Washington demanded that the Yemenis intensify their operations against AQAP and signalled preparedness to provide related military aid.

Initially, the support provided was relatively modest and limited to servicing of aging and outdated equipment of US-origin, like the remaining F-5s and the two C-130s. However, gradually, the value of aid provided by Washington increased, and by 2010 Yemen became the largest global recipient of funding from the US 'Train and Equip' program. Indeed, in late 2010, Sana'a was permitted to contract Bell Corporation for delivery of four UH-1H Huey II helicopters. A year later, the USA funded the training and establishment of the Counter-Terrorism Unit (CTU), and the acquisition of one CASA CN.235 light transport supposed to serve the same.

However, in his typical fashion, Saleh channelled most of the US aid into units commanded by his relatives: command of the CTU was assigned to Major-General Yahya Mohammed Abdullah Saleh, one of his nephews, while most of the US arms were stored instead of being distributed to the units for which they were intended. Foremost, Saleh remained unwilling to engage AQAP in an open war.[35]

Protests of 2011

By early 2011, Saleh's mismanagement of the country was too much for most of the Yemeni population: a series of mass protests against poverty, unemployment, and endemic corruption erupted all over the country. Initially, Saleh appeared unimpressed: the situation began to change when reports surfaced about several 'key military officers' turning against him.

Before long, it transpired that the officers in question were already at odds with Saleh from earlier times. Crucial amongst them was Ali Mohsen al-Ahmar: when Saleh ordered him to deploy his units on the streets and squash protesting, he disobeyed. Left without a solution, Saleh ordered the CSF, the CTU and the Republican Guards out to the streets. These repeatedly fired at protesters, killing dozens. Exploiting an opportune movement, Ahmar finally ordered his units out of their barracks – but only in order to position them between the loyalists and protesters – while presenting himself a 'protector of the pro-democracy movement'. On 24 March 2011, Ahmar went a step further and officially defected from Saleh, taking with him a number of high-profile military, political, and tribal leaders, foremost Sheikh Hamid al-Ahmar (chief of the Hashd Tribal Confederation, the Islah Party and the most powerful tribal leader of the country, closely linked to the Saudis). This was the move that signalled the beginning of the end of Saleh's rule over Yemen. With no end of mass demonstrations, the CSU & CTU taking the public heat for their increasingly violent crackdown, and nearly half of his military on the verge of armed mutiny, the President of Yemen was finally compelled to give up.

Following quite intensive combat operations against Houthis in the course of so-called Sa'ada Wars, of the 2004-2010 period, many of YAF's MiG-29s were in need of periodic maintenance. All of the related work was undertaken locally. This photograph shows a scene from one of the maintenance hangars at Daylami AB. (Pit Weinert Collection)

The united YAF inherited a small number of Mi-25/35 helicopter gunships from the former South Yemeni Air Force. Most were painted as seen on this example, in two shades of very dark grey (or even black) on top surfaces and sides, and light grey on the bottom of the fuselage and the boom. (via Albert Grandolini)

YAF against al-Qaeda

Because of Saleh's refusal to act against AQAP, his playing of the tribes, political parties, the USA and Saudi Arabia, and the ensuing chaos in the country, in early 2011 the Yemeni military effectively withdrew from much of southern and eastern Yemen. In turn, this left AQAP in a position to bring most of the Abyan and Hadramawt provinces under its control, and assault the town of Zinjibar.

The sole locally-based unit of the Yemeni Army – the 25th Mechanized Brigade – fought back with gusto, but suffered heavy casualties and was forced to withdraw and entrench within its base by 7 June 2011. For the next three months, Saleh's government largely ignored all of its calls for help: merely the YAF continued providing support in the form of air strikes and para-dropped supplies. As the number of reports about mistreatment of the local population by the AQAP continued to grow, the majority of military commanders and local tribal leaders became eager to confront the Jihadists.[36] Correspondingly, as soon as it was clear that Saleh was on the way out of the Presidential Palace in Sana'a, in early September 2011, a counteroffensive of three army brigades – the 31st, 119th, and the 201st – was organized. Attacking together with tribal levies, these not only lifted the siege of the 25th Mechanized Brigade in Zinjibar and liberated most of the area controlled by Jihadists in a matter of one week, but also caused such losses to the extremists that these took nearly four years to recover. Tragically, more than 280 army troops and at least 50 tribal levies paid the ultimate price for this victory, while another 600 were wounded.[37]

During this operation and afterwards, the YAF put AQAP under immense pressure through a series of air strikes. This enraged the extremists to a degree where they launched an outright assassination campaign against the air force – in addition to a campaign of suicide bombings of mosques perceived as 'Zaidi'. By October 2011, AQAP assassinated more than 30 YAF officers – usually by 'two masked gunmen on a motorcycle'. In May 2013, this campaign experienced a new quality when Major-General Nasser al-Jund, the commander of the YAF, appeared in the public to show pieces of a Su-22 that crashed on finals at Daylami AB – with bullet holes in them. Unknown at the time was that, because of subsequent developments in Yemen, the YAF would never get a chance to exact revenge.[38]

Two stills from a video showing a YAF An-26 that was damaged in an attack by AQAP on Daylami AB in April 2012. (Pit Weinert Collection)

The YAF's fleet of Su-22M-3s and M-4s suffered significant attrition during the Sa'ada Wars and immediately afterwards. This still from a video shows an example that was either shot down by the Houthis, or crashed, in October or November 2009. (Pit Weinert Collection

A Mi-171Sh – armed with gunpods and launchers for unguided rockets, navigating the terrain in the Hadramawt province, where the Yemeni army fought bitter battles against AQAP through most of the Year 2011. (Pit Weinert Collection)

Despite losses, 30 Su-22s (of which 18 were operational) survived the six Sa'ada Wars: 18 were still operational at the time this photograph of the example with serial number 2252 was taken, at Daylami AB, in 2011. (Pit Weinert Collection)

Table 1: Known, Claimed, and Confirmed YAF Attrition, 2001-2014[39]

Date	Aircraft	Pilot	Circumstances & Geographic area
17 Apr 01	F-5E	Captain Hallil az-Zindani killed	overshoot runway on landing and crashed, Sana'a
?? May 01	MiG-21bis	pilot ejected safely	
1 Mar 02	L-39C	crew killed	crashed on landing, Anad
8 Apr 03	L-39C	unknown	Aden
4 April 05	F-5E	pilot killed	Bayt Hadhal area, Sana'a
3 Jul 05	MiG-29	pilot ejected safely	crashed due to engine malfunction, Amran, Sana'a
9 Aug 05	An-26	1 killed, 22 injured	Mukalla
28 Aug 05	MiG-29	Capt Mohammad al-Hariri killed	crashed near ad-Duha, Hudaydah
15 Mar 06	unknown	2 killed, 1 injured	Dhamar
6 May 06	unknown	No injuries	destroyed in fire, Bani Matar, Sana'a
8 Aug 06	unknown	5 killed	hit mountain in Jayub area, Sana'a
7 Mar 07	MiG-29	pilot killed	crashed on landing at Sa'ada airfield
7 Mar 07	MiG-29	pilot ejected but injured	crashed on landing at Sa'ada airfield
3 Dec 07	Mi-171	pilot killed, fate of crew unknown	technical fault, Haraf Sufyan, Umran
2 Oct 09	MiG-21bis	1st Lt Shaban Ahmad Abdu Musleh killed	Marazen, Sa'ada
5 Oct 09	Su-22M-4K	pilot killed	No. 26 Squadron; claimed shot down by Houthis; Aland and al-Maqash, Sa'ada
8 Oct 09	Unknown	–	claimed as shot down by Houthis
8 Nov 09	Su-22M-4K	Capt Saleh al-Faqih ejected safely	No. 26 Squadron; claimed shot down by Houthis; Razen, Sa'ada, pilot recovered by helicopter two days later
7 Dez 09	MiG-21bis	pilot ejected safely	claimed as shot down by Houthis; Khaiwan, Amran
13 Jan 10	L-39C	crew ejected safely	crashed due to technical malfunction, Al-Braika, Aden
4 Feb 10	Su-22M-3	pilot killed	shot down, Juf
14 Feb 10	Helicopter	4 crewmembers killed	Kehlan, Sa'ada
10 Apr 10	MiG-21bis	Pilot ejected safely	technical malfunction, 7 July City, Hudaydah
20 Mar 11	Su-22M-3	Pilot killed	hit mountain in Juf area
20 Jul 11	Su-22UM	1st Lt Adel Nasser al-Qabati injured; Iraqi instructor injured	crashed on take-off from Hawban AB due to engine malfunction
28 Sep 11	Su-22M-4K	Capt Tawfik ad-Dabrai ejected safely, captured	Arhab, shot down by Islah Party militia
28 Sep 11	Su-22UM	crew killed (1 Syrian)	crashed on landing, Anad AB
13 Oct 11	3x Su-22	–	destroyed on the ground, unclear if sabotage or AQAP attack
13 Oct 11	F-5E	–	destroyed on the ground, unclear if sabotage or AQAP attack
1 Nov 11	Helicopter	–	caught fire and destroyed, Daylami AB
24 Nov 11	An-26	15 crewmembers and passengers killed	crashed due to technical malfunction, Sana'a; 8 of passengers were Syrian pilots
4 Jul 12	Mi-8	Capt Ali Mokbelya OK Capt Mohammed Nahari OK	damaged by ground fire, crashed in Sa'aba Governorate
15 Oct 12	MiG-21UM 2210	Col Atiq Mohammed Fara killed; 1st Lt Sidqi al-Amrani injured	crashed at Anad AB
17 Nov 12	Su-22M-4K	Col Mohammed Arkabi	damaged by ground fire over Hamdan; made successful emergency landing at Daylami
28 Nov 12	Mi-171Sh 2258	several crewmembers and passengers injured	damaged by ground fire in Sa'aba Governorate
19 Feb 13	Su-22UM 2224	Capt Mohammad Ali Naser Shaker ejected safely	crashed in western Sana'a, killing 12 on the ground
13 May 13	Su-22M-4K	Capt Ali Ajbadi Hani killed	shot down by AQAP, burst into flames and crashed inside Sana'a,
15 May 13	Mi-171Sh	Col Saleh Fawzy	hit by AQAP ground fire, no injuries reported
6 Aug 13	Mi-171Sh	Col Mohammed Abdullah Ahmad Qarazy, 3 crewmembers and 7 passengers killed	shot down by AQAP in Wadi Obeida area, Ma'rib
27 Aug 14	L-39C	Lt Muhammad at-Thabee ejected but killed	overshoot the runway at Anad

Hadi's Reorganization

Inked under severe pressure of the Gulf Cooperation Council – and especially Saudi Arabia – in November 2011, the deal for transition of power from Saleh and his proxies to a new government included a mandate for Major-General Abd Rabbu Mansour Hadi – an absolvent of the Frunze Military Academy in the former USSR, former officer of the South Yemeni Army, but meanwhile a Saudi protégé and Vice-President of Yemen – to take over as new President. Combined with the backing of the USA, this mandate emboldened Hadi to introduce sweeping reforms of all civilian, security and military authorities alike, aiming to purge them of Saleh-loyalists. Considering the number and influence of the latter, it was unsurprising that related decisions met tough resistance. Indeed, by the time Hadi assumed office, on 25 February 2012, at least 22 brigades – nearly a half of them elements of the Republican Guards – had already mutinied against his rule. As the new President continued his reforms, the stream of rebellions picked up: corroded by decades of corruption and severe fragmentation from within, most of the military began showing clear sings of insubordination.

The largest block created by this rift consisted of officers and other ranks loyal to, or affiliated with, Saleh – or at least his General People's Congress (GPC) party. While predominantly consisting of the Zaidis, this faction attracted a significant minority of the Shafi. In reaction to their mutiny, Hadi blocked the funding of, and limited all activity of, major units to a degree where all armoured and mechanized brigades were immobilized for lack of fuel and spares.

The majority of the YAF was already 'on barricades' too – but in protests against its commander, Major-General Mohammed Saleh al-Ahmar, Saleh's half-brother. Facing massive accusations for corruption and mismanagement, Ahmar resigned in April 2012 – though only after refusing to leave office for 19 days and threatening to shoot down any aircraft approaching Daylami AB, and thus Sana'a International. Although the majority of the YAF thus openly sided with Hadi and his Joint Meeting Parties (JMP), the president then reorganized the air force too. Flying units based at Daylami AB and all air defence brigades based in the Sana'a area were subjected to his direct control, while units deployed elsewhere around the country were subjected to the control of commanders of local Military Districts. Newly-established brigades of the YAF controlled squadrons that were sorted out by the origins of their equipment. The resulting Order of Battle for the YAF was as listed in Table 2.[40]

However, Hadi and his JMP never received widespread support from the population. On the contrary, the second largest faction within the military was the one led by Ali Mohsen and the Islah Party. The composition of the three blocks was as colourful as it could get. For example, while primarily consisting of the Shafi, Ali Mohsen's block also included Salafists, and was allied with a large number of Zaidi tribes from the northern highland. Indeed, although both Saleh and Mohsen hail from the Sanhan tribe of the Bakil tribal confederation, the majority of Mohsen's followers were from the Hashd tribal confederation. Correspondingly, the following conflict between these three blocks was foremost a conflict between top military, political and even economic figures of Yemeni society, and not an inter-tribal, inter-ethnic, or an inter-religious affair.

A still from a video documenting the sad fate of the An-26 that crashed outside Sana'a on 24 November 2011. Although the aircraft appears to have remained in reasonably intact condition, no less than 15 crewmembers and passengers – including 8 Syrian pilots – were killed. (Pit Weinert Collection)

After nearly 20 years of tough service in Yemen, only half a dozen F-5Es and F-5Bs remained operational with the YAF. This F-5B was photographed while climbing out of Daylami AB for some post-maintenance testing. (Pit Weinert Collection)

The MiG-29 fleet – down to about 30 airframes of which fewer than 20 were operational – remained the mainstay of the YAF until the bitter end. Through the period 2011-2014, the aircraft were frequently deployed for ground strikes on the Houthis and AQAP, usually armed with four B-8M pods for 80mm unguided rockets. (Pit Weinert Collection)

As Hadi continued reforming the military, protests and mutinies spread to a degree where even a number of crack units involved in fighting AQAP began abandoning their positions. Nevertheless, the president pressed on and next reorganized the three brigades equipped with surface-to-surface (or 'ballistic') missiles. According to Belarusian sources, as of 2013 the 1st Artillery Brigade still had ten operational 9M714 TELs, while the 26th Brigade still operated six 9P117M vehicles with similar purpose. Known stocks of missiles included 80 OTR-21s and R-17Es. However, the status of the 89th Artillery Brigade and its Hwasong-6 missiles remained unreported. That the latter unit remained operational became obvious only in July 2014, when President Hadi separated all three units from the disbanded Republican Guards, put them under the command of the Missiles Brigades Group (MBG), and re-designated them as the 5th, 6th and 8th Missile Brigades.[41]

The fate of the two C-130Hs donated to Yemen by the USA in 1979-1980 and operated by the 1st Squadron, YAF, was characteristic for the status of most of YAF's aircraft by 2013-2014: only one was operational, while the other was waiting for repairs estimated to cost around US$ 70 million – which Sana'a could not afford. (Tom Cooper Collection)

Table 2: YAF Order of Battle, 2013-2014

Unit	Base	Equipment	Remarks
CO YAF: Maj Gen Rashid Nasser al-Jund Chief-of-Staff: Maj Gen Malik az-Zuhairi			
II Military District	Mukalla		CO Maj Gen Muhsen Naser Qasem
190th AD Brigade	Riyan	SA-2	CO Brig Gen Yahya ar-Rusayshan
IV Military District	Aden		CO Maj Gen Nassir Abdu Rabbu at-Taher
39th Aviation Brigade	Anad	Z-242, L-39	
90th Aviation Brigade	Anad	MiG-21, Mi-8	CO Brig Gen Ali Atiq al-Ansi
120th Air Defence Brigade	Aden	SA-2, SA-3	CO Brig Gen Muhsen Mohammed al-Khabi
170th Air Defence Brigade	Bad al-Mandab	SA-2, SA-3	CO unknown
V Military District	Hudaydah		CO Maj Gen Mohammed Rajeh Labouza
67th Aviation Brigade	Hudaydah	MiG-21bis/UM, Mi-8	CO Staff Brig Gen Ali Yahya ad-Damin; incl. No. 6 Squadron
130th AD Brigade	Hudaydah	SA-2, SA-3, SA-6	
Directly reporting			
2nd Aviation Brigade	Daylami	F-5, C-130, Cessna 208, Huey II, Bell 206, Bell 212, Bell 214	CO Brig Gen Ahmed Mohammed ash-Shami[42], incl. 1st Squadron (C-130) & 2nd Squadron (F-5)
4th Aviation Brigade	Daylami	An-24/26, Il-76	CO Col Zaid Ali al-Akuwa
6th Aviation Brigade	Daylami	unclear	CO unknown
8th Aviation Brigade	Daylami	unclear	CO Brig Gen Omar Said Saleh
10th Aviation Brigade	Daylami	unclear	CO unknown
101st AD Brigade	Daylami	SA-2, SA-3, SA-6	CO unknown
110th AD Brigade	Daylami	Radar	CO unknown
140th AD Brigade	Sana'a	SA-2, SA-3, SA-6	CO unknown
160th AD Brigade	Sana'a	SA-2, SA-3, SA-6	CO unknown

Table 3: YAF's Aircraft & Helicopters, 2012-2014[43]

Aircraft Type	Number	Operational	Pilots	Bases
An-2, An-26	8	1	20	Daylami
Bell 206	3	1	?	Daylami
Bell 212	6	0	?	Daylami
Bell 214	3	0	?	Daylami
C-130	2	1	20	Daylami
Cessna 208	2	2	?	Daylami
F-5E & F-5B	12	6 (4 F-5E, 2 F-5B)	10	Daylami
Il-18	3	1	20	Daylami
L-39	24	20	-	Anad, Taiz
MiG-21	22	12	32	Anad, Hudaydah
MiG-29	30	10	15	Daylami, Anad
Su-22	30	18	60	Daylami, Taiz
Mi-8	10	7	30	Daylami, Taiz, Hudaydah
Mi-17	5	3	20	Daylami
Mi-171	8	8	15	Daylami, Aden
Mi-25	2	2	15	Daylami
UH-1H	4	3	?	Daylami

Houthis in Sana'a

During the protesting of 2011, the Houthis announced their support for demonstrators demanding Saleh's resignation. At the same time, they exploited the ensuing chaos to overrun and disarm, or force into submission dozens of tribes allied with the government. By 2012, they laid siege to the Shafi-majority town and religious centre of the Quietists in Dammaj. This was ended only two years later, when all the non-local Sunnis and all of the students were evicted to southern Yemen.

Meanwhile, the Houthis boycotted a single-candidate 'election' held in early 2012 with the aim of providing Hadi with a two-year term office. They did participate in the National Dialogue Conference – brokered by the UN and the Gulf Co-operation Council (GCC) with the aim of extending Hadi's presidency and authorising him to carry out additional reforms, but also of transforming Yemen into a six-region federal system – but withheld their support from the final accord. On the contrary, supposedly protesting Hadi's decision to increase fuel prices and cut diverse subsidies, the insurgents then clashed with units under the command of Ali Mohsen and finally launched an advance on Sana'a in early July 2014.

Initially, the YAF bombed some big columns of armed pick-up trucks (so-called 'technicals'), as these were underway through the Amran governorate and then approached the capital – reportedly causing a 'large number of casualties'.[44] However, out of concern for internal security and because of developments in Egypt, the government of Saudi Arabia then declared the Moslem Brotherhood as a terrorist organization and stopped supporting the Islah Party. With this party representing the centrepiece of the Saudi influence in Yemen, and its primary front against the Houthi movement in particular, much of the military ceased fighting. The insurgents were thus free to overrun Amran and the locally-based 310th Armoured Brigade, allied with Ali Mohsen, on 22 August 2014. While contemporary reports stressed the 'destruction' of this unit, the Houthis largely left it intact. Indeed, there are strong indications that the insurgents actually sought to avoid a direct confrontation with the military. Amongst others, the Houthis claimed that their operations would not target the army but, 'elements that are acting on partisan rather than national interests'. Correspondingly, they limited their action against the 310th to the arrest and summary execution of its commander, Brigadier-General al-Qushaibi – Ali Mohsen's close associate and the man the insurgents considered responsible for the death of their first leader, Hussayn al-Houthi, in September 2004. Rather unsurprisingly, their further advance was supported by some of the units that meanwhile mutinied against Hadi, while the block centred around Ali Mohsen and the Islah Party offered only token resistance. The YAF launched a few air strikes as the insurgents approached northern suburbs of Sana'a, on 17 and 18 September, but then ceased all combat operations as they encroached the Daylami AB. The Houthis thus found themselves in a position to bring the capital of Yemen under their control by 20 September 2014.[45]

The Houthi advance was not limited to Amran and Sana'a: they marched on the coast of the Red Sea and overran the Hudaydah area, by early October 2014, too. It was there that the Houthis came in control of three Su-22 fighter-bombers, later the same year.[46]

As soon as they took over, the Houthis forced Hadi to negotiate the so-called 'Peace and Partnership Agreement': this was planned to function as a power-sharing treaty between the government and insurgency, and end the violence. However, it was never honoured by either party: foremost the Houthis sabotaged it by running an outright man-hunt for members and allies of the Islah Party in the capital, and by imposing their control upon all the military units. When multiple commanders refused to obey orders and insisted on receiving these down regular chains of command, the insurgents reacted by appointing officers that sided with them instead. With the help of orders from the latter, they began encroaching even the 'restive' YAF.[47]

The air force resisted passively, while remaining elements of the military, the Presidential Guard, and surviving elements of the Islah Party's militia decided to fight. The violence in the Yemeni capital reached its peak on 19 January 2015, when the Houthis launched their final power grab. In two days of fighting, they drove the Presidential Guard out of the Presidential Palace and secured this complex, and then seized the Camp Bilad ar-Rus – the MBG's major base. Hadi was forced to resign – reportedly at gun-point – and put under house-arrest on 20 January 2015. A day later, the Houthis dissolved the parliament and on 6 February 2015 declared their Revolutionary Committee as the new government of Yemen.[48]

The last commander of the YAF, Major-General Rashid al-Jund, and his Chief-of-Staff, Major-General Malik az-Zuhairi, continued to resist until mid-February 2015, when they were dismissed and replaced by the Houthi favourites. This decision met such widespread disagreement within the air force that most of officers and other ranks subsequently abandoned their posts. The Yemeni Air Force thus practically ceased to exist.[49]

On 20 January 2015, the Houthis seized Camp Bilad ar-Rus, together with most of the ballistic missiles operated by the Missile Brigades Group of the Yemeni Army – including such as the R-17/Scuds seen in this photo from the mid-2000s. While unopposed by the units in question, this action signalled the start of the last chapter in the drama that resulted in destruction of the YAF. (Tom Cooper Collection)

A rare photo of four of about 48 TELs for 2K12 Kub (SA-6 Gainful) systems Yemen obtained in the 1990s. The personnel of most of the units equipped with this system seems to have sided with the Houthis/Saleh coalition by late 2014. (Pit Weinert Collection)

The Mess

The Houthi take-over in Sana'a – between September 2014 and February 2015 – resulted not only in the disintegration of the air force, but put the nail in the coffin of a unified Yemeni military. While of crucial importance for what happened in the country ever since, this development was largely ignored by the majority of international observers and the media, but especially by governments of a number of neighbouring nations that were about to become involved in this conflict. This is even more surprising considering Yemen's history of armed conflicts and military rule: the military intelligence agencies responsible must have warned their political masters that in a country where water sources are scarce, but arms as available in abundance, control over military units and bases (which in turn control water, stockpiles of arms, ammunition, spares, food, and fuel) is of crucial importance. Whether military intelligence services in countries like Saudi Arabia, United Arab Emirates, Egypt, or Kuwait did so or not remains unknown. What is certain is that as 2014 turned into 2015, Yemen military's allegiance to the central state virtually disappeared. Instead, different units sided with various private groups.

To make matters really complex, the rift within the military was not 'perfectly clean': by the time Saleh finally stepped down, in the period between September and November 2011, the military was split into three factions. Contrary to the explanations insistently published in the Western mass media ever since, the rift was never clearly defined solely by northern or southern backgrounds of the units in question, or their ethnic and religious and tribal affiliations. Not a few cases became known where elements of the same unit sided with different factions – each of which then continued the use of the old designation of the unit in question in order to emphasise its own legitimacy. Furthermore, and as since the initial mutinies of 2011, the identity of the officers in question played the key, but not the crucial role: while the majority of the Zaidis did side either with the Houthis or Saleh, up to one third of the officers to do so were the Shafi, or units predominantly staffed by the Shafi. Vice-versa: a large number of Zaidi officers, or units predominantly staffed by Zaidis, sided with other parties. Finally, a number of brigades declared their neutrality and remained locked inside their barracks. Precise details about most such units remain unknown to this day. The Yemeni military and society eventually split into the following blocks:

1. The Houthi network – meanwhile centred around two well-trained and equipped battalions of 'regulars', and a host of different militias totalling up to 20,000 regular combatants organized into the movement that designated itself the 'Ansar Allah' (Supporters of God) – attracted some Yemeni military commanders, and these took the whole, or parts of their units with them. Furthermore, the Houthis brought under their control most of the intelligence apparatus, including the National Security Bureau, headed by Abdullrabb Saleh Ahmed Jarfan.[50]
2. An even larger segment of the Yemeni military, and a major portion of tribes in northern Yemen, sided with the network orbiting around Saleh. Functioning along highly personal lines of loyalty, this block attracted foremost officers and units of the former Republican Guards, many of whom remained deeply disgruntled by Hadi's reforms.
3. The units still under the control of Ali Mohsen, most of the PSO, and various tribal militias affiliated with the Islah Party, created their own block that largely withdrew towards Ta'izz and Aden. As most of the military units in question disintegrated, some of their combatants regrouped to form so-called Popular Resistance militias.
4. Another block of forces to re-surface during the following months were the southern separatists of the so-called Hirak Movement. The origins of the Hirak can be traced back to 2007, when a peaceful protest movement aimed to call attention to the exclusionary policies of the elites that captured

A reconstruction of one of about a dozen MiG-21bis that were still in service with Anad-based 90th Aviation Brigade as of 2008-2009, by which time most of the fleet was overhauled in Ukraine. Its serial – 218 – identifies this aircraft as one of 60 MiG-21bis' acquired by former North Yemen in the period 1979-1982. Camouflage colours consisted of purple sand, olive green and chocolate brown on top surfaces and sides, and Light Admiralty Grey on undersides. Non-operational by 2011-2012, this MiG-21 was wrecked during the fighting for Anad AB in August 2015. It is shown armed with two types of bombs frequently deployed during the six Sa'ada Wars: FAB-250M-62 (inboard underwing pylon) and RBK-250 (outboard underwing pylon). It seems that roundels were applied only on the rear fuselage, and not on the wing. (Artwork by Tom Cooper)

Yemen was the only export customer for the Su-17M-4 – a variant originally manufactured solely for the Soviet Air Force. At least four such aircraft were acquired during or immediately after the war of 1994. While nothing is known about their look at earlier times, by 2008-2010 they wore different variants of this camouflage pattern, consisting of light brown and two shades of green on top surfaces and sides. Undersides were painted in Light Admiralty Grey. As usual by the time, the serial was based on the variant of the aircraft in question, followed by individual number. Serials of other variants of this family of aircraft included 401-424 for Su-22M-2s and Su-22UM-3s, 801-825 for Su-22M-3s and Su-22UM-3s, 601-625 and 2201-2245 for Su-22M-4s. Inset show the crest of the YAF – usually applied on the forward fuselage of every Sukhoi in service – and that of the 4th Aviation Brigade (which flew An-24/26 and Il-76 transports). (Artwork by Tom Cooper)

Over time, all of the YAF's MiG-29s were overhauled and brought to the SM-standard, and received the same camouflage pattern – consisting of beige and two shades of brown on top surfaces and sides, and Light Admiralty Grey on undersides. However, only 14 MiG-29SMs acquired from Russia between June 2002 and November 2004 received their markings applied in the fashion as illustrated here. These included the nick-name 'Shafaq' (the last light of the day or the red light after sunset) – applied in stylised Arabic on the forward fuselage, and in English on the fin – and a combination of the serial and the YAF crest on the intake sides. Furthermore, only these 14 aircraft received IFR-probes. The rest of the fleet had its serials and the YAF crest applied on the forward fuselage, and wore no nickname. The most frequently used armament consisted of B-8M pods for 80mm S-8K unguided rockets, but YAF MiG-29SMs are known to have deployed Kh-29 (AS-14 Kedge) guided air-to-ground missiles in combat too. (Artwork by Tom Cooper)

When the RSAF became involved in the Sixth Sa'ada War, in 2009, the majority of its Tornado IDS-fleet was still wearing the original, wrap-around camouflage pattern, applied since their delivery in the 1980s. This consisted of light stone, dark earth, and dark green. Their serials consisted of a 'prefix' indicating the unit in question (No. 75 Squadron in this case), and the aircraft's individual number. The unit patch was always applied directly below the fin flash. Notable is that most drop tanks in use as of that time were already painted in light aircraft grey. A similar colour was used on Damocles nav/attack pods, which were a relatively new appearance as of 2009. Notable also is that AIM-9M Sidewinder air-to-air missiles were always carried, regardless of the actual nature of the mission and a complete lack of aerial opposition. (Artwork by Tom Cooper)

During the second half of the 2000s, each of the RSAF squadrons operating Tornado IDS received four aircraft painted in Barley Grey overall. By 2015, this camouflage pattern was applied fleet-wide. Nevertheless, many of the underwing pylons and hardpoints, most of BOZ-101 chaff/flare pods (always carried under the outboard underwing pylon of the port wing), and Cerberus ECM-pods (always carried under the outboard underwing pylon of the starboard wing) were left in their original colours. Except for the national flag on the fin, and the serial applied in black colour (this still consists of a prefix indicating the unit to which the aircraft is assigned, and a two-digit individual aircraft number), all other insignia was toned down. A new appearance, introduced in the early 2010s, was the inscription 'God Bless You', usually applied in dark green on the forward fuselage. Since the Sixth Sa'ada War of 2009-2010, primary armament consists of Damocles nav/attack pods, and GBU-12 or GBU-49 guided bombs. Insets show the crests of Tornado-equipped Nos. 7, 75 and 83 Squadrons, RSAF. (Artwork by Tom Cooper)

All of the Saudi F-15S are painted in a relatively simple camouflage pattern consisting of Aggressor Gray (FS 36251) overall, with big splotches of Ocean Gray (FS 36176) along most exposed top surfaces. Their radomes are left in Gunship Grey (FS 36118) but weathering in different fashion than the rest of the fuselage. Except for the fin flash and unit crest, which are left in original colours, all other national insignia and serials, and most of maintenance stencils are applied in Aggressor Gray. Weapons configurations usually include GBU-12s and GBU-49s, AGM-65, and a wide range of general purpose bombs as well as CBUs. Regardless of the nature of the actual mission flown over Yemen, they are always armed with a pair of AIM-9Ms and AIM-120Cs each. This example from No. 55 Squadron is illustrated as configured for a reconnaissance sortie, in April 2015, and carries a Goodrich DB-110 reconnaissance pod under the centreline. Insets show the crests of Nos. 55 and 92 Squadrons, RSAF. (Artwork by Tom Cooper)

The UAEAF operates three squadrons equipped with 49 Mirage 2000-5 Mk IIs (also designated as the Mirage 2000DAD/EAD/RAD/9/9Ds). Most of these are painted in Bleu-Vert Pâle Satine (satin light blue-green) overall, with a standardised camouflage pattern in Gris Bleu Clair Satine (satin light ghost grey, similar to FS 25189 or FS 36375). Their radomes (made of composite material) are painted in Gris Clair (light grey, FS 36320). All wear a large crest of the UAEAF (& Air Defence) on the front fuselage, details of which are shown in inset. As well as air-to-air missiles like MICA and Magic Mk 2, they are armed with a wide range of guided air-to-ground weapons, all of which have been combat-tested in Yemen so far. Amongst these are (lower left corner) South African-designed and Emirates-assembled al-Tariq, and (lower right corner) Marconi al-Haqim (PGM-1), usually combined with the Thales Optronics TV/CT CLDP laser designator pod. (Artwork by Tom Cooper)

Equipped with the APG-80 AESA radar and F110-GE-132 engines, the F-16E/F Desert Falcons of the UAEAF belong to the most advanced variants of this series ever manufactured. All 80 are painted in a wraparound camouflage pattern consisting of light grey (FS 36495) and Light Ghost Grey (FS 36375). Serials – in the range 3001-3025 for 25 two-seat F-16Fs and 3026-3080 for 55 single-seat F-16Es – are always applied in dark grey on the fin only. Insets show the unit insignia of Shaheen Squadrons 1, 2, and 3 – the three units known to be operating F-16E/Fs. Most aircraft sighted in action over Yemen were single-seaters operated by Shaheen 1 Squadron (former No. 16 Squadron, which used to fly Mirage 2000s until 2007), though a few F-16Es from Shaheen 3 Squadron have been sighted in action since 2016 too. (Artwork by Tom Cooper)

This F-16E – apparently operated by Shaheen 3 Squadron, is shown together with some of heavier PGMs deployed by this type during the first two years of the Yemen War. These include GBU-31 (shown installed under the wing), al-Tariq, the AAQ-32 Sniper targeting FLIR and laser designator (usually carried on the right station under the intake on single-seaters, but often on the left side on two-seaters), al-Haqim (PGM-1), and AGM-84H. Other weapons known to have been deployed by Emirati F-16s include GBU-12, GBU-24, and GBU-49 LGBs, GBU-38 GPS-homing bombs, AGM-65 Maverick guided missiles, and also CBU-87, CBU-97, CBU-105 and other 'higher marks' of 'smart' cluster bomb units. (Artwork by Tom Cooper)

Kuwait originally announced the deployment 15 F/A-18C Hornets for operations over Yemen in March 2015. However, it seems that the number of aircraft present at Khamis Mushayt usually fluctuates between six and eight. Kuwaiti F/A-18s are operated by Nos 9 and 25 Squadrons (both home-based at Ahmed al-Jaber AB), and most are painted in this, wrap-around camouflage pattern, consisting of light gray (FS 36375), brown gray (FS 36307) and dark gray (FS 35237). In action over Yemen, most of these were sighted carrying either Mk.82 general-purpose bombs, or GBU-12/49 LGBs. Notable is that these are the only jets of the Saudi-led coalition still regularly armed with older AIM-7 Sparrow missiles (instead of latest AIM-120 ARMAAMs). Inset is shown the crest of No. 25 Squadron, KAF. (Artwork by Tom Cooper)

Bahrain maintains regular deployments of between four and six F-16Cs from Nos. 1 and 2 Squadrons, RBAF at King Khalid AB, since late March 2015, but next to nothing is known about their operations. All of the aircraft are painted in a unique, single-tone colour reportedly consisting 50:50 of FS 36622 and FS 35237. Most of aircraft from No. 2 Squadron are nowadays wearing a new paint scheme, in which the entire fin was painted in a slightly darker shade of grey colour, and then a big unit crest applied over most of the fin – as illustrated in the inset. It seems that by 2017 most of aircraft from No. 1 Squadron had received the same insignia. (Artwork by Tom Cooper)

Morocco acquired a total of 16 F-16C Block 52s and 8 F-16D Block 52s. These are operated by three flights (Escadrons) – Viper, Falcon, and Spark – of the Borak Squadron FRA. All are painted in sand (FS 33613) and dark earth (FS 30219; though with a strong red touch) on upper surfaces, and gray (FS 36270) on the radome and undersurfaces. The aircraft are known to have been delivered together with AIM-120C-7 and AIM-9M air-to-air missiles, AGM-65D/G/H Maverick air-to-ground missiles, GBU-10, GBU-12 and GBU-24 LGBs, and GBU-31 and GBU-38 GPS-homing bombs. However, in action over Yemen they are usually equipped with AAQ-32 Sniper targeting pods and GBU-12/49s, and carry four AIM-9M Sidewinders. (Artwork by Tom Cooper)

The Qatar Emiri Air Force deployed at least four of a total of nine Mirage 2000-5EDA single-seaters and three Mirage 2000-5DDA two-seaters from its No. 7 Air Superiority Squadron at King Khalid AB early during the campaign in Yemen. They are painted in same colours as Mirage 2000s of the UAEAF, and were observed in action over the Bab al-Mandeb area in 2016 again, usually armed with a pair of GBU-12/49s installed on a dual ejector rack under the centreline. One of the two-seaters was observed while wearing six mission markings (in the form of GBU-12-style silhouettes applied on the left side of the front fuselage), around the same time. (Artwork by Tom Cooper)

Despite reports about its supposed withdrawal from the Saudi-led coalition, the Egyptian Air Force continues deploying a detachment of F-16s to King Khalid AB on a regular basis, and these are still flying combat operations. Most examples sighted so far were F-16C Block 40s (illustrated here), drawn from the Abu Suweir-based 262 Tactical Fighter Wing, Gianclis-based 272 Tactical Fighter Wing, and Fayid-based 282 Tactical Fighter Wing. Egyptian F-16s are camouflaged in FS36270 and FS 36231 on top surfaces and sides, and FS 36375 on undersurfaces, but have large parts of the wing, centre fuselage and fin marked in orange (outlined in black) for easier identification. For operations over Yemen, they are usually armed with a single LANTIRN targeting pod, two GBU-12s or GBU-49s, and up to four AIM-9M Sidewinders. (Artwork by Tom Cooper)

Squadrons 1, 2 and 6 of the Royal Jordanian Air Force are flying a mix of refurbished F-16A Block 15s and former Belgian and Dutch F-16AMs (or F-16A/B Block 20 MLUs). All wear the standard camouflage pattern consisting of two grays (FS 36320 and FS 36118) on top surfaces, light ghost gray (FS 35375) on undersurfaces, and the radome in FS 36270, and have small black serials on the front fuselage and the top of the fin. Because of the slightly lower standard of their self-protection equipment, they usually also carry ALQ-131 electronic counter-measures pods under the centreline. Otherwise, their armament is generally similar to that of other F-16s used in the ongoing campaign in Yemen, and consists of AAQ-32 Sniper pods, GBU-12/49 LGBs, AIM-9M Sidewinder and AIM-120 ARMAAM missiles. (Artwork by Tom Cooper)

Sudan acquired a total of eight Su-24Ms from Belarus, via the company BelTechExport, starting in 2013. All were overhauled by the 558th Aircraft Repair Plant in Baranovichi before delivery, and received a desert camouflage scheme. While usually based at Wadi Sayyidna AB, between two and four are rotated to King Khalid AB outside Khamis Mushayt for tours of duty lasting three to four weeks since April 2015. Initially armed with FAB-250-230 general purpose bombs for operations over Yemen, shown on the main illustration, they are meanwhile known to have deployed GPS/GLONASS-assisted weapons too. The latter are based on Soviet/Russian FAB-250M-62-bomb-design, though modified by addition of kits designated 'Module-A', made in North Korea. (Artwork by Tom Cooper)

72 EF-2000s operated by Nos 3 and 10 Squadrons (crests shown inset, left upper corner), were initially deployed to fly CAPs over Yemen, armed only with German-made IRIS-T and US-made AIM-120 AMRAAM "Slammer" air-to-air missiles (insets in lower right corner). However, compatibility with Damocles targeting pods and laser-guided bombs like Paveway II and Paveway IV became available by April-May 2015. Ever since, the fleet – meanwhile reinforced through the addition of No. 80 Squadron – has seen intensive involvement in the Yemen War, not only in attacks on the Houthis, but against AQAP, too. Indeed, the only confirmed loss of a Saudi EF-2000 occurred on 14 September 2017, during combat operations against Islamic extremists in southern Yemen. (Artwork by Tom Cooper)

The crest of the 'Missile Force' of the Houthi/Saleh coalition and three illustrations depicting its primary weapons, from top towards the bottom: R-17E (Scud), Burkan-1 and Burkan-2 ballistic missiles. (Artwork by Tom Cooper)

EF-2000 from No. 80 Squadron, underway over the rugged terrain of northern Yemen, while armed with an IRIS-T air-to-air missile (outboard underwing pylon) and a Paveway II laser-guided bomb of British origin. (Fahd Rihan, via Mohammed Khalid)

All of the RSAF's KE-3As have been upgraded to the RC-135W-like standard, including the addition of plenty of aerials, large housings for SLARs in 'cheeks' and a bigger radome. (Photo by Ahmed Hader)

An AH-64A of the United Arab Emirates Air Force firing an AGM-114 Hellfire guided missile during an attack on the Houthi positions along the Red Sea coast, in January 2018. (UAE MOD)

An AMX-56 Leclerc MBT of the Emirati Task Force deployed in south-western Yemen in December 2017. (Courtesy WAM)

Two 155mm G-6 howitzers of South African origin, operated by Emirati ground forces, during the fighting against the Houthis in the Mocha area in south-western Yemen in December 2017. (Courtesy WAM)

A CH-4 Wing Loong (Pterodactyl I) UCAV of Chinese origin, as seen in service with the RSAF. (Photo by Ahmed Hader)

key government and military positions since the unification of 1994 came into being. While remaining particularly popular in southern cities, this movement spread from Aden to al-Mahra and began addressing broader grievances such as the appropriation of southern land and resources. Although never truly united, representatives of the Hirak objected the National Dialogue Conference almost as fiercely as the Houthis did. The Hirak and the Houthis attempted to negotiate but their relationship soured in early 2015 as the latter advanced on Aden, pushing southern separatists into an uneasy alliance with Hadi.[51] Ironically, most of the foreign media subsequently declared the southern separatists unilaterally, yet wrongly, as 'Hadi loyalists', although the centrepiece of their ideology is an independent state in southern and/or eastern Yemen.

5. It was in the latter part of the country that another block of forces came into being as of late 2013. The block in question is affiliated with the Hadramawt Tribal Confederation (HTC) – another segment of Yemeni population systematically marginalized by Saleh's administration. In December 2013, the HTC found itself at odds with Hadi's government over the killing of its leader – Sheikh Sa'ad Bin Habrish al-Hamuumi. In reaction to its demands for the killers to be handed over and that all the security services for oil companies operating in Hadramawt to be taken over by the local tribes (instead being run by corrupt military commanders), the government declared the movement as 'allied with AQAP', and turned down all of its requests. Following the failure of two rounds of negotiations, the HTC launched an armed uprising that resulted in all the land access routes to oilfields in Hadramawt province blockaded, forcing a large-scale suspension of exploration.

   To make related affairs even more complex, since 2012 Hadramawt was frequently hit by strikes flown by US-operated UAVs. While US attacks on AQAP gangs found at least muted approval of the HTC, they repeatedly hit innocent civilians and caused much distress to the population, in turn – and quite logically – prompting Hadramis to put all the blame upon Hadi's government.

6. Considering the worsening security situation in the country and their similar political aims, it is unsurprising that some parts of the HTC and the southern separatists entered into cooperation in 2014. Thus came into being the Liberation Brigades of the South (LBS) – a group that initially operated against Yemeni Army, and then against AQAP. Ironically, because the HTC, LBS and the Hirak were all demanding independence for this part of the country, and such a state was in Saudi Arabia'a strategic interest of constructing a southern pipeline to the Gulf of Aden for its oil exports, these groups attracted significant amounts of support from Riyadh and from Abu Dhabi. Unsurprisingly, by 2014 Hadramawt was hopelessly out of control of any kind of central government of Yemen.[52]

7. Finally, while generally not contesting Hadi's government, the Quietists established a notable presence in Aden and Ta'izz, from where they began operating not only against the Houthis, but against AQAP too. Over time, their combat effectiveness was to convert them into one of most important allies of the foreign intervention in Yemen.

Houthi Ministry of Defence

Following extensive negotiations, the Houthi and Saleh networks entered an alliance of convenience during the autumn of 2014.[53] By mid-February 2015 they established their own chain of military command, the Supreme Security Council (SSC). During the following two weeks, the SSC appointed 10 new generals to crucial positions. Correspondingly, what was left of the YAF by this time came under the command of Rashid al-Jund, officially appointed the 'Commander of the Aviation Affairs'. This position was supported by a number of 'advisors' and 'deputies': al-Jund's top advisor became Abdallah al-Harazi, the precise function of whom remains unknown. Other known top commanders included Ali ad-Dhameen (CO Hudaydah AB and the locally-based flying units); Abdelrahman al-Wathri (CO Anad AB and locally-based units, meanwhile re-organized as the 'Aviation and Air Defence College'); and Ahrya ar-Rowaishan (CO Air Defence Affairs and thus in command of all ground-based air defence units and units equipped with early warning radar systems). Through orders issued by these and other newly-appointed officers with similar backgrounds, by early March 2015, the SSC established itself in control of up to 50% of the Yemeni military, as described in Table 4.[54]

Considering the content of hundreds of different reports from the period between September 2014 and April 2015, the conclusion is that out of 88 known brigade-sized units of the Yemeni military, no less than 46 sided with the Houthi/Saleh Coalition, 5 with Hadi, 3 with southern separatists, 3 were overrun by AQAP, while the status of 30 others remains unknown. For all practical purposes, this meant that Hadi – who already lacked his own political base in the country – now lost all semblance of support from the military.[55]

Determined to complete the take-over of the entire country, the SSC then began developing plans for an all-out-advance on southern Yemen. For this purpose, it reorganized the military forces and Houthi militias under its control. Precise details about the resulting organisational structure remain unknown, but it is

One of the last signs of the YAF's activity: a still from a video showing an Il-76TD transport about to land at Daylami AB on 22 March 2015. According to unconfirmed reports, the aircraft was involved in hauling reinforcements and supplies for forces of the Houthi/Saleh coalition. (Yemeni Internet)

known that the SSC generally grouped its units into three types of formations depending on their origins and equipment:

- Conventional military units left over from the Yemeni Army and commanded by officers that sided with the Houthi/Saleh coalition were generally deployed in urban areas;
- The majority of special forces units, former Republican Guards units, and artillery units were generally deployed along the border to Saudi Arabia; while
- most of the remaining units – a mix of Houthi militias and remnants of former Yemeni Army units – were deployed elsewhere, foremost in the south.

Table 4: Dissolution of the Yemen's Military, September 2014 – April 2015[56]

Unit	HQ/Base	Last known or newly-appointed Commander	Notes
Hadi Minister of Defence: Maj-Gen Mahmmoud Subaihi Houthi Minister of Defence and Chief of the General Staff: Brigadier-General Naji Qairan (appointed 25 March 2015) Houthi Deputy Chief of the General Staff: Major-General Zakaria Mohammed ash-Shami			
I Military District	Sayun, Hadramawt	Maj-Gen Abdul Rahman al-Halili	Halili sided with Hadi
37th Armoured Brigade	Camp al-Khasha'a, Hadramawt	Maj-Gen Abdul Rahman al-Halili	unit sided with Hadi
115th Armoured Brigade	Camp Thamud, Hadramawt	Brig-Gen Ahmed Ali Hadi	unit sided with Hadi
23rd Mechanized Brigade	Camp al-Abr, Hadramawt	Brig-Gen Hamoud Naji Daras	unit overrun and disarmed by AQAP
11th Border Guard Brigade	Camp tar-Rumah, Hadramawt	Brig-Gen Saleh Timis	Initially sided with southern separatists, then with Hadi
135th Infantry Brigade	Camp al-Qatan, Hadramawt	Brig-Gen Yahya Mohammed Abu Awja	status unclear
II Military District	Mukalla, Hadramawt	Maj-Gen Muhsen Naser Qasem	
27th Mechanised Brigade	Riyan AB (Mukalla)	Brig-Gen Abdulaziz Qaid ash-Shamiri	unit overrun and disarmed by AQAP
190th Air Defence Brigade	Riyan AB (Mukalla)	Brig-Gen Yahya ar-Rusayshan	unit overrun and disarmed by AQAP
123rd Infantry Brigade	Camp al-Hat, Mahrah	Brig-Gen Abdullah Mansour	unit sided with Hadi
137th Infantry Brigade	Mahrah	Col. Mohammed Yahya al-Qadi	status unclear
1st Naval Infantry Brigade	Socotra	Col Ahmed Abdul Wali ad-Dhahab	**Dhahab sided with Houthis/Saleh, new commander appointed but unit status unclear**
III Military District	Ma'rib	Maj-Gen Ahmed Saif Muhsen al-Yafa'i	**Yafa'i sided with Houthis/Saleh**
13th Infantry Brigade	Camp Sahn al-Jin, Ma'rib	Brig-Gen Ali Mohammed al-Faqih	declared neutrality
14th Armoured Brigade	Camp Sahn al-Jin, Ma'rib	Brig-Gen Mohsen ad-Da'ari	**parts of the unit sided with Houthis/ Saleh**
180th Air Defence Brigade	Camp Sahn al-Jin, Ma'rib City	?	**sided with Houthis/Saleh**
2nd Navy Infantry Brigade	Belhaf, Shabwah	Admiral Qasem Rajeh Labouza	**sided with Houthis/Saleh**
2nd Mountain Infantry Brigade	An-Nusaybah, Shabwah	Brig-Gen Ahmed Saleh al-Hamzi	**sided with Houthis/Saleh**
3rd Mountain Infantry Brigade	Ma'rib	Brig-Gen Mansour Ali A'id	Reportedly disbanded on 22 May 2013, but active in 2015; sided with Hadi
19th Infantry Brigade	Bayhan, Shabwah	Brig-Gen Hamid as-Somali	**base overrun by AQAP, heavy weapons taken away; many troops sided with Houthis/Saleh**
21st Mechanized Infantry Brigade	Ataq City, Shabwah	Brig-Gen Mohammed Hussein al-Jamaa'i	**sided with Houthis/Saleh**
107th Infantry Brigade	Safir, Ma'rib	Brig-Gen Khaled Nasser Yaslim	status unclear
312th Armoured Brigade	Sirwah, Ma'rib	Brig-Gen Abdu Rabbu ash-Shadadi	sided with Hadi
IV Military District	Aden	Maj-Gen Nasir Abdu Rabbu at-Taheri	
15th Infantry Brigade	Zinjibar, Abyan	Col Mohammed Ali al-Muazeb	**most of elements with all heavy weapons re-assigned to 115th Brigade and thus sided with Houthis/Saleh**
17th Infantry Brigade	Camp Dabab, Bab al-Mandab	Brig-Gen Saleh Muhsen as-Sabari	**sided with Houthis**
22nd Armoured Brigade	Camp al-Janad, Ta'iz	Brig-Gen Hamoud Ahmed Dahmash	**partially sided with Houthis/Saleh, partially fighting against them**
31st Armoured Brigade	Anad AB, Lahij	Brig-Gen Abu Bakr Faraj al-Atiqi	sided with southern separatists
33rd Armoured Brigade	Dhaleh, Dhaleh	Brig-Gen Abdullah Dhabaan	**sided with Houthis**
35th Armoured Brigade	Camp Mocha, Ta'iz	Brig-Gen Mansour Muhsen Ahmar	sided with Hadi

Unit	HQ/Base	Last known or newly-appointed Commander	Notes
39th Armoured Brigade	Camp Badr, Khormaksar	Brig-Gen Mehdi Shaklia	**partially sided with Houthis/Saleh**
39th Aviation Training Brigade	Anad AB, Lahij	Col Saleh Tamis	**partially sided with Houthis/Saleh**
90th Aviation Brigade	Anad AB, Lahij	Brig Gen Ali Atiq al-Ansi	**partially sided with Houthis/Saleh**
111th Armoured Brigade	Ahwar, Abyan	Brig Gen Mohammed Hussein al-Bukhaiti	neutral but fighting against AQAP
115th Infantry Brigade	Camp Hazem, al-Jawf, but deployed in Shaqra Disttrict, Abyan	Brig Gen Mohammed Abdullah ash-Shamba	**sided with Houthis/Saleh**
120th Air Defence Brigade	Aden	Brig-Gen Muhsen Mohammed al-Khabi	de-facto disbanded and non-operational
170th Air Defence Brigade	Bab al-Mandab	Brig-Gen Abdullah al-Haddad	**sided with Houthis/Saleh**
201st Mechanized Infantry Brigade	Anad AB, Lahij	Brig-Gen Marzouk Mohammed Sayadi	status unclear
V Military District	Hudaydah	Maj-Gen Mohammed Rajeh Labouza	
2nd Border Guards Brigade	Haradh, Hajjah	Brig-Gen Ali Amr A'ata	sided with southern separatists, then with Hadi
25th Mechanized Infantry Brigade	Abs District, Hajjah	Brig-Gen Ali Jazaa Ahmed Hydra	status unclear
67th Aviation Brigade	Hudaydah AB	Brig Gen Ali Yahya ad-Damin	**sided with Houthis/Saleh**
82nd Infantry Brigade	Camp as-Salif, Hudaydah	Col Omar Jawhar	**sided with Houthis/Saleh**
105th Infantry Brigade	al-Malahaidh, Hajjah	Brig-Gen Abdul Karim as-Sayadi	status unclear
121st Infantry Brigade	al-Khawkhah, Hudaydah	Col Faysal Qasem Saleh Jabari	**sided with Houthis/Saleh**
VI Military District	Amran	Maj-Gen Yahya Ghaleb al-Hawiri	
1st Artillery Brigade	Sa'ada	Brig-Gen Sadiq Ali Sarhan	**sided with Houthis/Saleh**
29th Mechanized Infantry Brigade	Camp Harf Sufyan, Amran	Brig-Gen Hafizullah Ahmed Yahya as-Sadmi	status unclear
72nd Infantry Brigade	Camp harf Sufyan, Amran	Brig-Gen Saleh al-Hamasi	status unclear
101st Infantry Brigade	Camp al-Buqa, Sa'ada	Brig-Gen Abdul Wahhab Abdu Rabbu Qashim	**sided with Houthis/Saleh**
103rd Infantry Brigade	Sa'ada	Brig-Gen Omar Mohammed Abdullah	**sided with Houthis/Saleh**
122nd Infantry Brigade	Sa'ada	Brig-Gen Abbas Abdullah Mus'ad	**sided with Houthis/Saleh**
125th Infantry Brigade	Sa'ada	Col Muhsen al-Harmali	**sided with Houthis/Saleh**
127th Infantry Brigade	Sa'ada	Col Jihad Ali Antar	**partially sided with Hadi, rest with Houthis**
131st Infantry Brigade	Camp Kitaf, Sa'ada	Brig-Gen Fadal Hassan Mohammed	**sided with Houthis**
133rd Mountain Infantry Brigade	Sa'ada	Brig-Gen Saleh al-Mayuf	**partially sided with Hadi, rest with Houthis/Saleh**
310th Armoured Brigade	Amran	Brig-Gen Qushaibi (KIA August 2014); Maj-Gen Subaihi (Mar 2015)	CO KIA by Houthis in August 2014; unit withdrawn and re-organized in Anad area, early 2015
VII Military District	Dhamar	Maj-Gen Ali Mohsen Ali Muthanna	
26th Mechanized Infantry Brigade	as-Sawadiyah, al-Bayda	Brig-Gen Khaled Ali Mohammed al-Jaifi	**sided with Houthis/Saleh**
30th Armoured Brigade	Camp Hamza, Ibb	Brig-Gen Mohammed Hajab	status unclear
55th Artillery Brigade	Yarim, Ibb	Brig-Gen Mohammed as-Sayani	status unclear
117th Mechanized Infantry Brigade	Camp al-Mukayras, al-Bayda	Brig-Gen Ali Ahmed al-Hayani	**sided with Houthis/Saleh**
139th Mechanized Infantry Brigade	Rada'a, al-Bayda	Col Ahmed Abdul Wali Mohammed ad-Dhahab	status unclear
203rd Mechanized Infantry Brigade	Ibb	unknown	status unclear
Presidential Protection Forces	Sana'a	Brig-Gen Saleh Mohammed al-Jaeemalani	
1st Presidential Guard Brigade	Sana'a	Brig-Gen Saleh Mohammed al-Jaeemalani	**sided with Houthis**
2nd Presidential Guard Brigade	Sana'a	unknown	**sided with Houthis**

Unit	HQ/Base	Last known or newly-appointed Commander	Notes
3rd Presidential Guard Brigade	Sana'a	unknown	**Sided with Houthis; equipped with T-80s**
314th Armoured Presidential Guard Brigade	Sana'a	Brig-Gen Hussein Muhsen al-Maqdad	possibly re-organized as the 4th Armoured Brigade
Defence Reserve Forces	Camp Sawad, Sana'a	Maj-Gen Mohammed al-Jaifi	Jaifi sided with Houthis
4th Armoured Brigade	Anad AB, Lahij	Brig-Gen Mohammed Abdullah as-Sayaghi	**sided with Houthis/Saleh**
7th Infantry Brigade	Khawlan, Sana'a	Brig-Gen Taher Sabran Qasem	status unclear
61st Artillery Brigade	Camp As-Sawad, Sana'a	unknown	**sided with Houthis/Saleh**
62nd Mechanized Infantry Brigade	Camp al-Farijah, Sana'a	Brig-Gen Khalid al-Jaifi al-Main	status unclear
63rd Mechanized Infantry Brigade	Camp Bani Jarmouz, Sana'a	unknown	status unclear
83rd Artillery Brigade	Sana'a	unknown	status unclear
89th Infantry Brigade	Camp Haffa, Sana'a	Brig-Gen Mohammed Ali Sanad	status unclear
102nd Mountain Infantry Brigade	Al-Jumaymah, Sana'a	Brig-Gen Hamid at-Tawiti	status unclear
Ghamdan Brigade	Sana'a	Brig-Gen Ahmed al-Ansi	**sided with Houthis/Saleh**
Strategic Reserve Forces		Brig-Gen Majali Mijidia al-Muradi	
1st Mountain Infantry Brigade	Sana'a	Brig-Gen Mohammed Ahmed al-Jaradi	**sided with Houthis/Saleh**
10th 'Storm' Brigade	Bajil, Hudaydah	Col Salim Muhsen Musad Zarman	**sided with Houthis/Saleh**
Missile Brigades Group		Brig-Gen Mohammed Nasir Ahmed al-Atefi	
5th Missile Brigade		Col Mansour Abdullah Hussein at-Tarmah	overrun by Houthis
6th Missile Brigade	Camp Faj Attan, Sana'a	unknown	**sided with Houthis/Saleh**
8th Missile Brigade	Camp Sabra/Bilad ar-Rus, Sana'a	Col Masoud Ahmed Hussein al-Ghabash	**sided with Houthis/Saleh**
Balance of the YAF			
101st Air Defence Brigade	Daylami AB	unknown	**sided with Houthis/Saleh; also known as 'Radar Brigade'**
110th Air Defence Brigade	Daylami AB	unknown	**sided with Houthis/Saleh**
140th Air Defence Brigade	Sana'a	unknown	**sided with Houthis/Saleh**
160th Air Defence Brigade	Sana'a	unknown	**sided with Houthis/Saleh**

CHAPTER 4
STORM OF RESOLVE

Dramatic events continued rattling Yemen through mid-March 2015: on the 20th, a Yemeni group affiliated with the so-called 'Islamic State' (colloquially 'Daesh' in the Middle East) bombed three mosques in Sana'a, killing more than 150 people. Amid the ensuing chaos, Hadi escaped from house-arrest in Sana'a to his birth-town of Aden, rescinded his resignation in the course of a TV-appearance and declared himself the legitimate president.

Abdul Malik al-Houthi, the leader of the Houthis, reacted with the announcement of a general mobilisation, stressing it was 'imperative' to defeat AQAP and its affiliates – among whom he counted Hadi. In a last-ditch attempt to secure Aden, Hadi then put all that was left of loyal armed forces in the city under the command of his Minister of Defence, Major-General Mahmmoud Subaihi. In turn, Subaihi was captured by the Houthis and transferred to Sana'a, on 23 March 2015.[57]

Realizing that the situation was beyond the point of becoming critical, Hadi and his entourage then fled from Aden to Saudi Arabia: on 24 March he re-appeared in Riyadh during a meeting with the Saudi Defence Minister, Crown Prince Mohammad bin Salman as-Saud. Immediately afterwards, Hadi called on the UN Security Council to authorize, 'willing countries that wish to help Yemen to provide immediate support for the legitimate authority by all means and measures to protect Yemen and deter the Houthi aggression.' A day later, Hadi's foreign minister, Riad Yassin, officially requested military assistance from the Arab League.[58]

These developments made the leaders of the Houthi/Saleh coalition determined to complete their take-over of Yemen before anybody could react. Bolstered by dozens of army units that sided with them, they were in a reasonably good position to achieve most of this objective: for a while at least, it appeared as if nothing would stand in their way. It was at that point in time that the Saudi government decided to launch a military intervention and thus became embroiled in a war the outcome of which remains anything other than predictable. Ever since, the resulting conflict has been fought on multiple frontlines, primarily on the ground, but very much in the air and at sea too. In most of cases, operations on different frontlines were not directly related: at most, the only common link between them is the omni-presence of air power of the Saudi-led coalition of Arab states.

Advance in the South

The advance into southern Yemen of the Houthi/Saleh coalition began on 18 March 2015, when the Ashoura Battalion – one of two 'regular' Houthi units, equipped with about a dozen each of T-55s and BMP-1s, and a host of technicals – suddenly appeared at Anad AB, where some YAF personnel and the officers of locally-based army units sided with it. Two days later, a video surfaced on the internet purportedly showing 'Houthi personnel' while operating one of air force's Zlin Z-242 trainers from this air base: the personnel in question were actually YAF cadets that sided with Saleh. However, most of the personnel of the 90th Aviation Brigade actually ran away and disappeared, and thus the 21 MiG-21 fighter-bombers of this unit remained on the ground.

Early on the morning of 19 March, a battalion of the Special Guard commanded by General Abdul-Hafez as-Saqqaf – who sided with the Houthi/Saleh coalition – secured the Aden International Airport (IAP). In turn, Saqqaf's troops were routed by elements of the 39th Armoured Brigade that remained loyal to Hadi, and the militia of the Hirak movement, on the next day, and the General forced to flee to Sana'a.[59]

On 21 March 2015, Hadi escaped from house-arrest in Sana'a to his birth-town of Aden, and appeared on the TV to declare himself the legitimate president. The Houthi/Saleh coalition reacted by accelerating its advance in multiple directions – and some of the efforts in question even received air support. At Daylami AB, the SSC bribed one MiG-29 and two-Su-22 pilots of the YAF to fly combat sorties for them. These flew three air strikes against the Presidential compound in Aden later during the day. Local army units opened fire with anti-aircraft guns – perhaps fired a few SAMs too – and thus prevented two of the involved pilots from making their second bombing runs.[60] Such actions remained an exception to the rule: on the contrary, most of the YAF personnel never returned to their positions. The last known action of the YAF was to scramble a few MiG-29s from an unknown air base to fly patrols for protection of the presidential compound in Aden early on 25 March. However, they disappeared after most of the 39th Brigade sided with Houthis and recaptured the international airport.

Meanwhile, on 22 March, the Ashoura Battalion reached Ta'izz, where it encountered very little resistance. On the contrary, approximately half of the 35th Armoured Brigade sided with it. In turn, after most of the local security forces had refused to carry out his orders, Hadi's governor of Ta'izz, Brigadier-General Hamoud al-Harthy, resigned. Two days later, other columns of the Houthi/Saleh coalition entered the port of Mocha, on the Red Sea, and the town of Dhale, where the 17th Infantry and the 33rd Armoured Brigade sided with them, respectively. Reinforced – and supported by several Mil Mi-17 helicopters of the YAF – the Houthis then opened a headlong charge for Aden, and reached the outskirts of this port on the morning of 25 March.[61]

Combatants of the Ashoura Battalion with two T-55 MBTs. (Yemeni internet)

Hadi's entourage and foreign diplomats about to embark on a vessel that brought them out of Aden, early on 24 March 2015. (Yemeni internet)

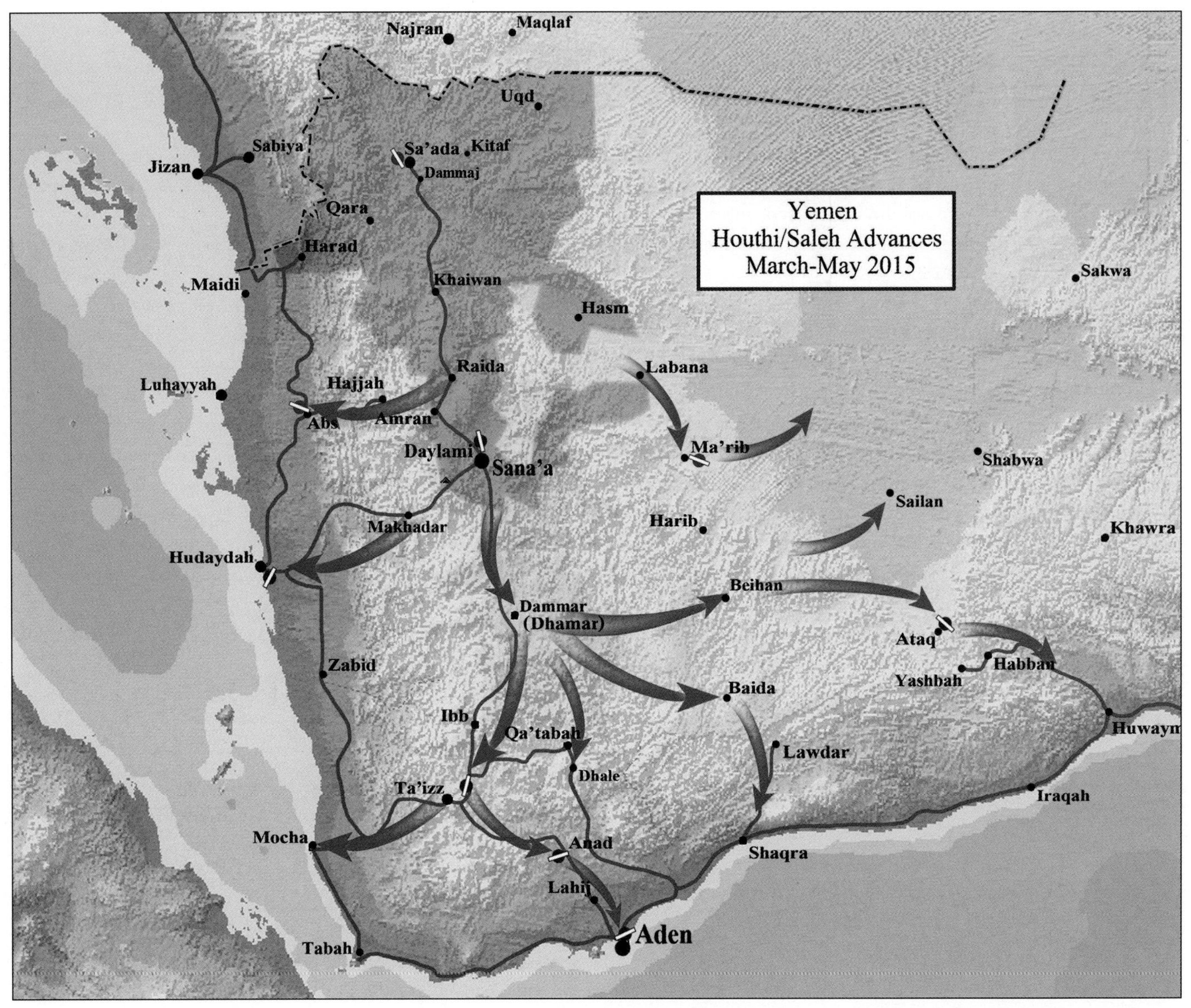

Map 2 The area controlled by the Houthi/Saleh coalition as of mid-March 2015, and their advances into western, southern and central Yemen of the following two months. (Map by Tom Cooper)

Battle for Aden

By 27 March 2015, forces of the Houthi/Saleh coalition had encircled Aden and then – reinforced by elements of the 33rd Armoured, 115th Infantry, 117th Mechanized Infantry, and parts of the 39th Armoured Brigades – pushed into the city centre. It was here that they experienced their first serious reverse in the course of this campaign. Heavy, sustained and precise air strikes of the Saudi-led coalition guided by Emirati special forces operators deployed on the ground (see next chapter), hit the assailants very hard and forced them to disperse along minor streets. This in turn bought the time for various of the local militias to concentrate and launch an outright manhunt, killing or capturing dozens. After regrouping, the Houthi/Saleh forces launched a headlong advance into the city centre on 29 March, but then came under artillery fire from warships of the Saudi-led coalition deployed off the coast, and further air strikes. Dozens of combatants, and even more civilians, were killed in battles that meanwhile raged all the way from Zinjibar via Khormaksar to Aden International and the port, before the Houthis – supported by several tanks – took control of the Crater District and the Presidential Palace. It took two days of intensive air strikes, and heavy casualties amongst defenders on the ground to dislodge them from this area and force them to withdraw.[62]

After regrouping, the Houthi/Saleh force resumed its advance on 5 April, by making a detour around the eastern outskirts of Aden before taking several neighbourhoods in the centre. The Hirak and AQAP militias caused them heavy losses during the fighting for Mualla District, where at least three MBTs were knocked out. Nevertheless, on 8 April, the Houthi/Saleh forces pushed into the Crater District, supported by at least one tank and two other armoured vehicles: this assault collapsed only under sustained air strikes and naval bombardment. Combined with the presence of Emirati special forces and air drops of supplies, air strikes enabled the local militias to secure the complex of the presidential palace by 13 April and then push the Houthi/Saleh forces out of Khormaksar on the next day. With this, the situation in Aden stabilized for a while.

To accelerate its advance southwards, the Ashoura Battalion made extensive use of commercial tilt-trailers for transportation of heavy weapons. This truck was photographed while hauling a BMP-1 into Ta'iz on 21 or 22 March 2015. (via Tom Cooper)

Significant numbers of Ratel armoured personnel carriers of South African origin (here the variant with turret-mounted twin 23mm cannon) were deployed by Yemen Army units that sided with the Houthi/Saleh coalition. (Yemeni Internet)

Saudi Planning

Stubborn resistance of local militias and the remnants of military units still loyal to Hadi were not the only reason for the defeat of the Houthi/Saleh alliance in Aden. Much more important proved the Saudi decision to heed Hadi's calls for help. After declaring the Houthis to be 'Iranian proxies', officials in Riyadh issued an ultimatum on 24 March, demanding that the insurgents withdraw from Sana'a within three days, leave all heavy weapons behind, permit Hadi to return and restore himself in power, and return to negotiations. When the Houthis turned this ultimatum down, the Saudis launched their intervention.

Although the Saudi military was not officially put on alert by that date, and related political decisions appear to have been taken in a hurry, related military preparations had already been going on for some time: indeed, a meticulously prepared plan for a military intervention in Yemen had been in development for a number of years.[63]

Based on experiences from the campaign of 2009-2010 and US experiences from campaigns in Iraq of 1991 and 2003, the plan in question became possible thanks to a substantial reform of the Saudi military. According to unofficial Saudi sources, military prisons in Saudi Arabia rapidly filled after the end of the intervention in Yemen of 2009-2010 – primarily with people who, 'skirted the system to promote their family members and friends'. All promotion on the basis of loyalty and nepotism was cancelled, and a strict system of promotion on the basis of merit and skills introduced instead. More importantly, the entire doctrine of national defence was overhauled. While emphasising bolstered defences of northern and western parts of the country at earlier times – because of confrontations with Israel and Iraq – the requirement to defend the southern border were acknowledged and these significantly reinforced.[64]

Planning for the Saudi offensive operations in Yemen envisaged the establishment of complete aerial dominance, denial of the Yemeni air defences and surface-to-surface missiles to the Houthi/Saleh coalition, -and also the destruction of major military bases, petrol/oil/lubricant (POL) depots, and maintenance facilities. Another set of targets included so-called 'leadership targets': top political and military commanders of the Houthi movement and the GPC, but also major state institutions. The aim of this campaign was not only to destroy enemy leaders, but foremost to make the effective function of their authorities impossible.[65]

Royal Saudi Air Force in 2015

The RSAF – which had played a dominant role already during the campaign of 2009-2010 – was vastly expanded in the course of the following years. The already large fleet of McDonnell-Douglas/Boeing F-15C/D/S Eagle/Strike Eagle interceptors and strike fighters, and PANAVIA Tornado interdiction-strikers (IDS), was meanwhile supported by 6 Boeing E-3A Sentry airborne early warning and control systems (AWACS), 5 Boeing KE-3A tankers and 3 RE-3A ELINT/SIGINT-gathering aircraft, and about 40 C-130H transports and KC-130H tankers. Since 2015, additional orders were placed for a total of 85 F-15SAs (and an upgrade of all existing F-15s to similar standard), 72 EADS EF-2000 Typhoon II fighter-bombers (or Typhoon FGR.Mk 50 and T.Mk 51, although it seems these designations were not in use), 30 C-130Js and 5 KC-130Js.

The wing structure was bolstered to a degree where each wing received between two and four flying units, a weapons and tactics school (or corresponding training facilities for other purposes), and a maintenance squadron. Intensive and realistic training with multiple allied services from abroad, and with similar equipment, enabled the air force to reach high degrees of commonality with the USAF and the US Navy, and run joint combat operations in Syria, in 2014 and 2015.

During the years immediately before the start of their intervention in Yemen, the Saudis went to great extents to decrease the number of foreign advisors working with their armed forces. While as of 2009-2010 up to 4,000 employees of various British companies alone were still working for the RSAF, by 2015 their number was greatly reduced: units flying Tornados and Typhoons were meanwhile down to only between two and four employees of British Airspace (BAE) assigned to them, for example. Theoretically, all of these were working as 'advisors', but their primary task was that of helping the Saudis solve any kind of major technical issues. Contrary to earlier times – and with the exception of foreign officers serving official exchange tours in Saudi Arabia – no foreign contract pilots flew for the RSAF anymore. The largest concentration of foreigners remained a group of between 50 and 60 US, and about a dozen British and French military observers assigned to the High Command of the air force: between six and ten of these were assigned directly to the RSAF's Air Operations Centre in Riyadh. Nominally, these officers – with the rank of Colonel or Lieutenant-Colonel (or equivalent) – served as 'military attachés' to the local embassies, but in practice they were involved in planning and actively advising the RSAF with regards to combat operations, acquisitions and logistics. In comparison, Saudi intelligence agencies – like the Intelligence Department of the RSAF – remained heavily supervised by US and British personnel, even though Saudi officers always had the final say. The only other major group of so-called 'ex-pats' serving with the RSAF are the cleaning personnel: most of these are Filipinos, but some Bangladeshis are present too.[66]

Overall the result of the Saudi efforts and investment was that as of March 2015, the RSAF had four fully operational flying wings ready for war in Yemen, with another one working up and ready to provide detachments. The No. 5 Flying wing, based at Khamis Mushayt (King Khalid AB), included Nos 6, 55, and 92 Squadrons equipped with F-15S'. The No 11 Flying Wing, based at Dhahran (King Abdul Aziz AB) included Nos 7, 75 and 83 Squadrons equipped with Tornado IDS – all upgraded to Tornado GR.Mk4-standard. Furthermore, No. 2 Flying Wing, based at Taif (King Fahd AB), was in the process of working up Nos 3 and 10 Squadrons equipped with Typhoon FGR.Mk 50 and T.Mk 51 fighters, while Nos 15 and 80 Squadrons were still in the process of converting to this type.[67]

Combat support aircraft were provided by No 6 Flying Wing, based at al-Kharj (Prince Sultan AB), including E-3A Sentries from No 18 Squadron, KE-3As and RE-3As from Nos 19 and 23 Squadrons, and SAAB 2000s from No 66 Squadron. The only component upon which the RSAF remained short were tanker aircraft: No 24 Squadron (from No 6 Flying Wing) was still working-up on four Airbus A.330 multi-role tanker transport (MRTT) aircraft. Therefore, KE-3As and KC-130J tankers were in heavy demand early during the following campaign.

As well as the acquisition of new aircraft, Saudi Arabia invested heavily into establishing domestic production for most of the necessary ammunition and thus launched production of such precision guided munitions (PGM) as GBU-12 and GBU-49 laser-homing bombs.

While the air force was to play a dominating role in the following conflict in Yemen, the RSLF was to play a very important role too. Meanwhile expanded into four aviation groups and reinforced through the addition of 94 AH-64 Apache attack helicopters, 13 Bell 406 scout helicopters, and 37 Sikorsky UH-60L transport helicopters, the Saudi army aviation's – and that of the Royal Saudi National Guards' aviation, which is operating the newest AH-64Es – primary task was the support of border defences.

Little Sparta

The most important RSAF ally in the skies over Yemen became the United Arab Emirates Air Force (UAEAF). The United Arab Emirates (UAE) is a federation of seven sheikhdoms that had been a British protectorate for decades before being released into independence in 1971. The forces merged together into a national military force during the US-led war against Iraq, in 1991. Ever since, the Emirates have run close cooperation with Western militaries, in particular. Correspondingly, the UAE deployed troops to Kosovo as part of the NATO-led peacekeeping force, starting in 1999; special forces troops to Afghanistan to support the US-led war against the Taliban; detachments of the UAEAF in support of the NATO-led operations over Libya, in 2011, and the US-led coalition fighting the so-called 'Islamic State' in Syria. Today, the UAE's military not only closely cooperates with that of the USA, but hosts contingents from multiple Western forces at its military bases. While the port of Jebel Ali serves as the biggest port of call for the US Navy outside the USA, the UAEAF operates the largest air warfare training centre in this part of the world, at the Dhafra AB.[68]

Crafted out of essentially 'nothing', immense investment into equipment and training of this air force over the last 40 years resulted in one of the best-equipped and best-trained flying military services in this part of the World. Since the mid-2000s, the UAE entered into cooperation with multiple private military companies to build up its military, and in 2014 introduced mandatory military service for all Emirati males between the ages of 18 and 30, and optional training for all women.

The centrepiece of the UAEAF is four units operating the survivors of the original 80 Lockheed-Martin F-16E/F Fighting Falcon fighter-bombers (reported follow-up order for 25 additional examples from 2014 appears never to have materialised) and three units operating survivors from a total of 68 Dassault Mirage 2000-5 MkIIs (originally delivered in variants Mirage 2000DAD/EAD/RAD/9/9Ds, but meanwhile all brought to Mirage 2000-9 standard). Combat aircraft are supported by two Saab 2000 AEW&C aircraft, eight Boeing C-17ER Globemaster III and six C-130H transports. The air force's Group 18 includes a Special Operations Squadron equipped with AH-64D Apache, CH-47D Chinook and UH-60L/M Black Hawk/Battlehawk helicopters, while much of the remaining helicopter fleet was separated from the UAEAF and grouped within the 10th Army Aviation Brigade (equipped with AS.550C3 Fennec, Bell 407s, AH-64A/Ds, and other types).

In addition to acquiring aircraft and helicopters, the UAEAF developed an extensive training infrastructure – centred around the Khalifa Ibn Zayed Air College in Abu Dhabi – and purchased a huge arsenal of the most modern, custom-developed guided weapons of US, French and South African origins, some of which are meanwhile assembled at home in the UAE. Like the RSAF, since the start of its operations in Yemen, the UAEAF began operating a significant fleet of different UAVs, too.

Saudi F-15S have flown most of the combat sorties over Yemen to date. This example (serial 617 from No. 6 Squadron) was photographed while returning from a combat sortie to Khamis Mushayt AB in April 2015. Notable is the armament consisting of a Sniper targeting pod (underneath the left intake), the GBU-49 LGB next to it, as well as AIM-9M (inboard side of the underwing pylon) and AIM-120C air-to air missiles. (Photo by Fahd Rihan, via Mohammed Khalid)

A row of Tornado IDS strike-fighters of No. 75 Squadron, RSAF. Notable is the Damocles navigational/targeting pod under the example in front. (Photo by Fahd Rihan, via Mohammed Khalid)

An RE-3A of No. 19 Squadron, RSAF as seen during take-off, shortly before the war. All have meanwhile received further upgrades, which brought the standard of their equipment close to that of USAF's RC-135W ELINT/SIGINT-gatherers. (Photo by Fahd Rihan, via Mohammed Khalid)

The latest type to enter service with the RSAF is the EF-2000 Typhoon. This example (serial 1019) from No. 10 Squadron, was photographed during a training mission in 2017. (Photo by Fahd Rihan, via Mohammed Khalid)

An F-16E of the UAEAF, armed with (from right to left) AIM-120C AMRAAM and AIM-9M Sidewinder air-to-air missiles, GBU-49 laser-homing bomb, drop tanks and a Sniper targeting pod, rolling for take-off for its next combat sortie over Yemen. (Photo by Fahd Rihan, via Mohammed Khalid)

An F/A-18C of the Kuwait Air Force as seen at Khamis Mushayt AB in April 2015. (Photo by Fahd Rihan, via Mohammed Khalid)

A Su-24M of the Sudanese Air Force as seen at Khamis Mushayt AB in May 2015. Notable is the armament consisting of six FAB-250-200 general purpose bombs. (Photo by Fahd Rihan, via Mohammed Khalid)

Allied Air Forces

Other air forces to join the Saudi-led coalition and deploy combat and combat-support aircraft to Saudi Arabia since late March 2015 were as follows:

- Royal Bahraini Air Force (RBAF), which provided up to 12 F-16C/D Block 40 fighters;
- Egyptian Air Force (EAF), which provided 8-12 F-16C/D Block 40 and Block 52 fighters;
- Royal Jordanian Air Force (RJAF), which provided 6 F-16AM fighter-bombers;
- Kuwait Air Force (KAF), which provided up to 15 Boeing F/A-18C/D Hornet fighter-bombers, and C-17 Globemaster IIIs and C-130J Super Hercules transports;
- Royal Moroccan Air Force (also *Forces royales air*, FRA), which provided 6 F-16C/D Block 50 fighter-bombers;
- Qatar Emiri Air Force (QEAF), which provided 10 Mirage 2000-5EDA/DDA fighter-bombers and interceptors, and C-17A Globemaster IIIs and C-130J Super Hercules transports; and
- Sudanese Air Force (SuAF), which provided small detachments (usually two aircraft) of Sukhoi Su-24M strike fighters.

Most of the aircraft in question were forward deployed at Khamis Mushayt for tours of duty lasting between three and four weeks. Ever since, aircraft and crews of all of the air forces involved have gone to great lengths to not only provide as many of their personnel as possible with combat experience in Yemen, but also to keep these crews fresh. Correspondingly, aircraft and their crews are regularly rotated in and out of theatre of operations.

Demonstrating the multi-national character of the Saudi-led coalition, this long row of F-16s shows the fins of (from foreground towards rear) Emirati, Bahraini, Moroccan, and Egyptian aircraft – all simultaneously based at Khamis Mushayt as of May 2015. (via Tom Cooper)

Two F-16AMs from No. 2 Squadron of the Royal Jordanian Air Force undergoing final checks before another combat sortie over Yemen in April or May 2015. (via Mohammed Khalid)

As in 2009, the Saudi armed forces established a highly effective joint headquarters for all the branches of their military, and all the allied air forces, with its own air planning cell responsible for coordinating all the aerial operations over Yemen.

Opening Blows

The first air strikes of what became known as the Operation Decisive Storm (an alternative translation is 'Storm of Resolve'), run by the Saudi-led alliance – involving about 100 combat, and up to 50 combat-support aircraft of the RSAF and the UAEAF – took place around 0200hrs local time on 26 March 2015. In the course of the following two hours, F-15s, F-16s, and Tornado IDS' bombed the positions of seven air defence brigades – each comprising between four and eight SAM-sites equipped with SA-2, SA-3, and SA-6 systems that were under the control of the Houthi/Saleh coalition. Also hit was the sole Yemeni radar brigade deployed in the Sana'a area, and dozens of homes of top Houthi officials and military officers that sided with them.

The second wave followed in the early hours of the morning and was slightly shorter. It targeted the Presidential Palace and the HQ of the Central Security Agency in Sana'a, and several bases of Yemen Army units south of the capitol. Elsewhere, the RSAF bombed Houthi bases in Malaheez and Hafr Sufyan, the airport of Sa'ada and weapons depots around the town, the Tariq Hawban AB outside Ta'izz, and the nearby base of the 22nd Armoured Brigade, Anad AB, the 180th Air Defence Brigade deployed near Ma'arib, and the base of the 33rd Armoured Brigade in Dhaleh. Later during the day, the RSAF flew the third wave of air strikes, and targeted suspecting hideouts of Abdul Malik al-Houthi and other insurgent leaders in the Sa'ada area. In addition to objects with an obvious military purpose, the Saudis demolished the Hussein Badr al-Houthi shrine outside Sa'ada – a building sacred to the Houthis – and then different Houthi positions in Shada'a and Baqem districts of the Sana'a, both of which are predominantly populated by the Zaidis, killing at least 25 civilians in the process. Finally, aircraft of the Saudi-led coalition bombed several concentrations of Houthi/Saleh forces along the border – often from relatively low altitudes.

Initial reports about the results of these attacks were rather controversial: at Daylami AB, Saudi and Emirati bombs destroyed a number of large hangars housing equipment provided by the USA to fight AQAP – including a recently-delivered CASA CN.295 light transport and a Beechcraft Super King Air. Heavy damage was caused to a Bell 412 and an UH-1H – both of which were stored due to lack of spares. While the Houthi/Saleh propaganda instantly exploited this, claiming that the Saudis were flying 'air strikes in support of the al-Qaeda', the fact was that the intention was to knock out aircraft and helicopters that the Houthi/Saleh coalition might have been able to return to service, and deliver a 'message' to the YAF – to stay out of the fight. Tragically, a number of PGMs either malfunctioned or outright missed their targets: the bombing of Daylami AB alone resulted in the deaths of 23 civilians that lived in neighbouring apartment buildings. Although officials in Sana'a claimed no fewer than three Saudi- and one Emirati fighter bombers as shot down, the coalition suffered no losses.

During the second night of Operation Storm of Resolve, the RSAF continued striking pre-selected targets – foremost air defence sites and major military bases – in Sana'a, Hudaydah, and Sa'ada. Verified reports confirmed hits on 15 different locations in the Sa'ada area alone, where at least 10, probably 12 civilians were killed too. Attacks on air defence positions of the Houthi/Saleh coalition were very effective. The majority of radars operated by Yemeni air defence brigades were knocked out within the first 48 hours of attacks. Nevertheless, these managed to fire a number of SAMs. While it is unlikely that an aircraft as advanced as the F-15S was shot down by obsolete SAMs operated by the Houthi/Saleh alliance, Riyadh subsequently confirmed that the crew of one of its F-15S was forced to eject over the Red Sea, where it was recovered by Sikorsky MH-60 Pave Hawk special operations helicopter of the USAF, operated from Djibouti. The exact reason for this loss remains unknown: the Saudis claimed that the aircraft went down due to a mechanical failure – also cited as the official reason for every single loss of aircraft or helicopters flown by the Saudi-led coalition in this war ever since. Furthermore, as soon as Khartoum announced its decision to deploy four Sukhoi Su-24M fighter-bombers in support of the Saudi-led coalition, the Houthi/Saleh coalition claimed to have shot down one of the 'Sudanese Sukhois'.

Daylami AB was one of the principal targets for air strikes flown during the night of 27 to 28 March, when the Saudis cratered the runway in several places. A large column of Houthi/Saleh forces was then hit during the afternoon of 28 March in the Hudaydah area, as was another moving from Aden towards Mukalla.

Late in the evening of the same day, the first round of air strikes on the bases of the MBG was flown. Another wave struck the same bases on the night of 29 to 30 March 2015, and officials in Riyadh subsequently claimed the destruction of 21 missiles. It was only weeks later that the Saudis grudgingly admitted that the 'Houthis' (actually units of the Yemen Army that sided with the Houthi/Saleh coalition) had managed to scatter and hide most of the TELs and missiles before these could be hit. Indeed, it was on 30 March 2015, that the 'Houthis' attempted to fire one of the SS-1s in direction of Saudi Arabia. However, the missile malfunctioned and crashed.[69]

On 29 March, the Saudi-led coalition bombed Daylami AB again: supported by several groups of Houthi militiamen, the remaining YAF personnel repaired the damage with quick-drying cement, and subsequent reports from Riyadh indicated at least some aerial operations. In between air strikes, and as soon as the runway was operational again, foreign airliners were granted permission to evacuate expatriates out of Sana'a (for example, two Russian aircraft evacuated 290 people on 3 April). However, such opportunities were exploited for the activity of the few YAF aircraft operated by personnel that sided with the Houthi/Saleh coalition, too. As far as is known, these included at least one flight by a Yemen air force Ilyushin Il-76TD transport, and several flights by helicopters that were used to haul reinforcements, ammo and supplies to the south. It seems that such action eventually prompted the RSAF to knock out most of the sun-shelters used to protect MiG-29s – the pride of the YAF – and F-5Es parked at Daylami, during the night to 30 March 2015.[70]

A completely destroyed and burned out MiG-29SM of the former Yemeni Air Force, as seen after one of many air strikes on Daylami AB, flown in March, April and May 2015. (Pit Weinert Collection)

Wreckage of the SNR-75 ('Fan Song') fire-control radar of the S-75M (ASCC-code 'SA-2 Guideline') SAM-site assigned to the 180th Air Defence Brigade in Ma'rib, as seen after an air strike on 26 March 2015. Ironically, this site was deployed for the protection of an oilfield exploited by the US company Haliburton. (via A. N.)

Typhoons in Combat

According to official Saudi releases, RSAF flew no fewer than 1,200 sorties during the first three days of operations over Yemen. For weeks afterwards, it maintained an operational tempo of 120-150 combat sorties a day. The primary reason for such intensity of operations was not only the pre-war planning to hit and knock out crucial military installations, but also the necessity to simultaneously provide close air support (CAS) to their own or allied units involved in fighting the Houthi/Saleh coalition on multiple frontlines. Furthermore, transport aircraft of the RSAF flew missions during which supplies of arms, ammunition and food for forces fighting against the Houthi/Saleh coalition in Aden were para-dropped.

Indeed, the original list of targets in Yemen was exhausted rather quickly: Sa'ada Airport was re-attacked for the fifth time, Daylami AB and the SA-6 SAM-site assigned to the 130th Air Defence Brigade in Hudaydah were re-attacked for the third time during the night from 31 March to 1 April 2015. Therefore, the Saudis subsequently re-directed their aerial campaign against the major bases of Yemeni military units that had sided with the Houthi/Saleh coalition, and then to the neutralisation of whatever was left of the Yemen Air Force. Correspondingly, air bases in Sana'a, Hudaydah and Ta'izz were repeatedly attacked until the Saudi Ministry of Defence declared 70% of the YAF combat aircraft destroyed.

Some of the air strikes in question were flown by brand-new EF-2000 Typhoon fighter-bombers of the RSAF. Namely, finding out about the EF-2000's potential in this role, the Saudis had, since 2013 scrambled to take over the initiative in relation to further development of this type's air-to-ground capabilities from the RAF. Using Damocles pods to self-designate for British-made Paveway II laser-guided bombs (LGBs), they have progressively improved the performance, reaching the ability to self-designate before the British did so. This became possible because the RSAF – as soon as it was briefed on the Typhoon's 'Future Capability Roadmap' – offered its funding for further research and development, enabling time-scales to be significantly compressed. Instead of working-up through the usual process – related to companies like NETMA, QinetiQ, and then the RAF – the Saudis pushed hard to develop the capabilities on their own, not only with regards to self-designation for PGMs, but with regards to air-to-air gunnery too. Eventually, they took an early variant of the Phase 1 Enhancement (P1E) software and used this to achieve an earlier operational capability. The result was that as soon as No. 10 Squadron RSAF had 12 single-seaters and 6 two-seaters in service (all from Tranche 2), and enough crews qualified to fly them as multi-role platforms, the unit began flying combat sorties in Yemen.[71]

A RSAF EF-2000 Typhoon armed with Paveway IV laser-homing bomb, parked inside a hardened aircraft shelter at King Khalid AB. (Ministry of Defence of Saudi Arabia)

A row of Yemeni SS-1C TELs with R-17E missiles as seen on a pre-war parade in Sana'a. (Pit Weinert Collection)

Spectacular photograph showing results of air strikes on MBG bases in suburbs of Sana'a on 29 March 2015. (Pit Weinert Collection)

CHAPTER 5
MULTI-FRONT WAR

Initially during its intervention in Yemen, the Saudi-led coalition entrusted ground operations to local allies backed by special forces and air strikes. In Aden, this combination proved perfectly sufficient, but elsewhere, various Yemeni groups proved not only poorly trained, but disorganized and disunited too. Indeed, when a combined force of Emirati army troops and Yemeni allies launched the highly successful operation Golden Arrow in the aftermath of securing Aden, the resulting advance created a giant power vacuum behind the frontlines – within which the Jihadists of AQAP roamed freely. Furthermore, during May and June 2015, the Houthi/Saleh coalition launched a series of small but often spectacular – and widely publicised – attacks on the Saudi border, creating the impression that the entire military might of the Saudi-led coalition was entirely useless. Combined, these and other factors resulted in the Saudi and Emirati decision to stop their own offensive operations and buy time to organize a new, coherent Yemeni military force that would fight for Hadi (and, of course, for Saudi and Emirati interests).

Securing Aden

Early during the Saudi-led military intervention in Yemen, it was foremost the situation in Aden that remained of greatest concern for military commanders in Riyadh. After its forces lost the Presidential Palace complex, on 13 April, and were forced to withdraw from Khormaksar, a day later, the Houthi/Saleh coalition attempted to reinforce its units again in mid-May. The operation in question was run via Dhaleh, and resulted in the coalition's next major setback of this war: not only were several of its convoys ambushed by tribal fighters, but the 33rd Brigade disintegrated under severe air strikes, causing its commander and survivors to flee towards the north on 1 April 2015. The Houthi/Saleh coalition re-attacked and captured Dhaleh later in the month, but was finally forced out on 20 May.[72]

On 23 May 2015, different militias and AQAP launched an attack into the Mansourah District of Aden, followed by one of the Hirak into Khormaksar on the next day. According to local sources, these two operations were coordinated by the new, 'pro-government' governor, Nayet al-Bakri. By 25 May 2015, the Houthi/Saleh forces were forced out of districts of Sheikh Othman, Dar Sa'ad and Salah ad-Din, and the Oil Port. The remaining Houthis then entrenched at the international airport and in northern Aden.[73]

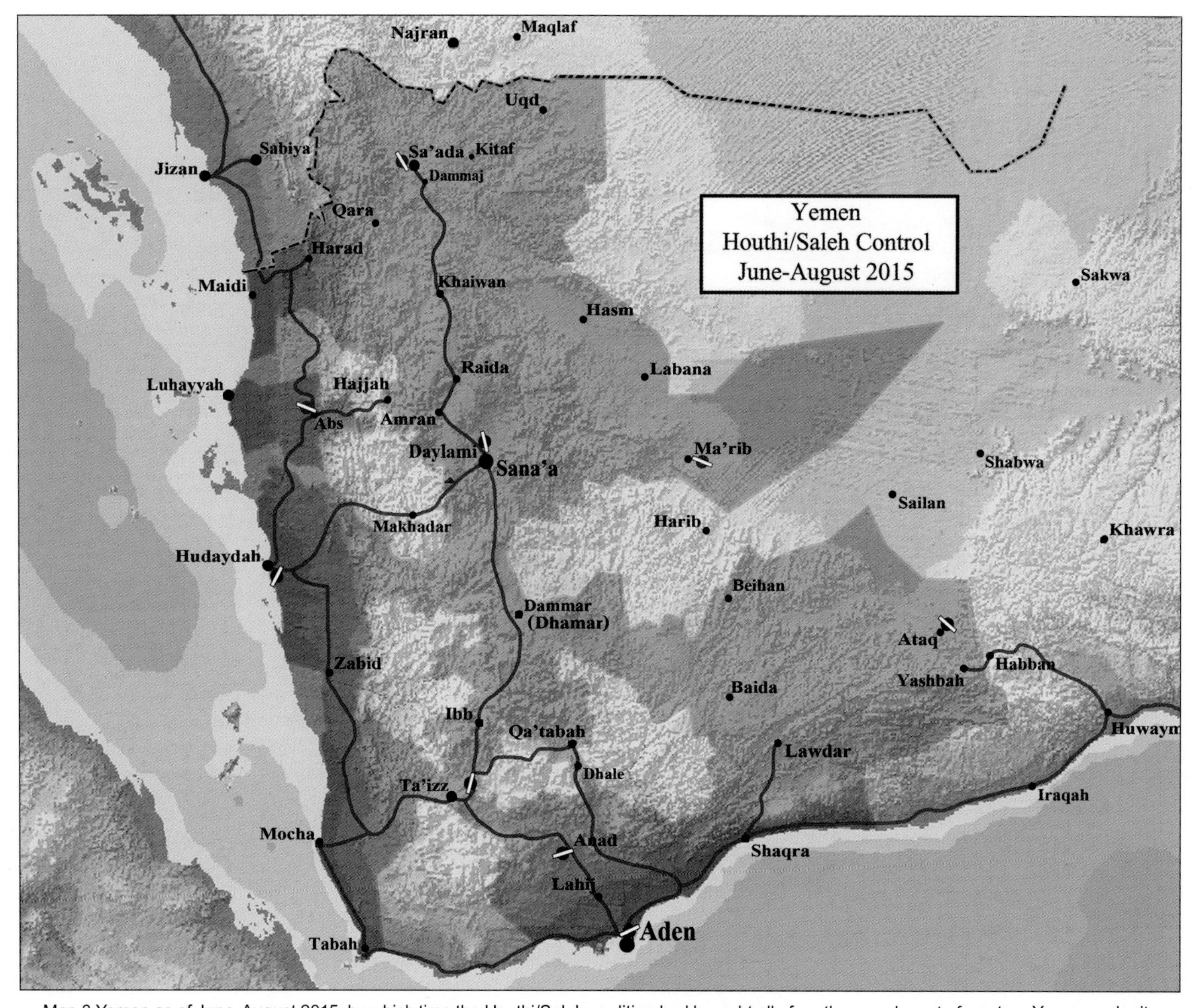

Map 3 Yemen as of June-August 2015, by which time the Houthi/Saleh coalition had brought all of northern and most of western Yemen under its control. Notable is that sizeable mountainous areas in between were still held by a range of other parties involved in this conflict. (Map by Tom Cooper)

Operation Restoring Hope

Late on 21 April 2015, officials in Riyadh suddenly announced that all the objectives of Operation Storm of Resolve had been met and that this enterprise was over. While widely perceived as an end of air strikes, the intervention went on: on 23 April, the Saudis explained they would 'continue preventing the movement of Houthi militias or undertaking any operations inside Yemen'. Indeed, before long it became clear that the government in Riyadh had merely re-named its operation into 'Restoring Hope'.[74]

On 28 April 2015, the Saudi-led coalition re-attacked Daylami AB and the civilian side – Sana'a International: this time it destroyed not only the YAF Il-76 transport that was used to haul reinforcements and supplies for Houthi/Saleh forces in the south, but also – and for unknown reasons – a privately-owned Bombardier CRJ (Canadair Regional Jet) business jet. Furthermore, this attack was reportedly flown in order to prevent an Iranian Airbus loaded with medical aid from landing there. Certainly enough, the latter was intercepted by a pair of RSAF F-15C Eagles (armed with, amongst others, the vaunted AIM-9X Sidewinder air-to-air missiles), and forced to return to Iran shortly after entering Yemen's airspace. Something similar happened with an Algerian Il-76 that attempted to bring a load of medical supplies to Yemeni capital.

An F-15S landing at Khamis Mushayt AB after another sortie over Yemen. Notable is the Goodrich DB-110 reconnaissance pod installed under the centreline (see the colour section for further details). (via Mohammed Khalid)

Meanwhile, political manoeuvring of the Saudi-led alliance resulted in some movement on the diplomatic plan. However, during the UN-negotiated cease-fire between 11 and 16 May 2015, the Houthi/Saleh coalition managed to rush their last contingent of reinforcements (a column of more than 50 vehicles, including several BM-21s) – via Lawdar to Aden. Simultaneously, additional artillery units were deployed to Ta'izz. These two operations eventually prompted the Saudi-led coalition to resume hostilities. Shortly after midnight of 18 May 2015, a series of air strikes hit Sana'a, this time targeting ammunition depots in the mountains surrounding the city (foremost Nuqom, which was hit at least 10 times), and several residential areas. Furthermore, Saleh's house in Sanhan District was demolished. Elsewhere, air strikes targeted Sa'ada and Hajjah in the north, but also Houthi/Saleh positions in Aden, and then Ibb, Ta'izz, and Ma'rib.

On 19 and 20 May 2015, the Saudi-led coalition flew uninterrupted air strikes on targets in the Sana'a area, repeatedly targeting multiple military bases and storage depots – such as the one at Mount Nuqom – but also a football stadium in the south of the city. Further attacks prompted the Houthi/Saleh coalition to claim to have shot down a 'Saudi F-16' over Bayt Khayran area – in the district of Bani Harith, north of Sana'a – at 0215hrs local time on 23 May 2015. Although announcing that they were sending 'dozens of fighters to find the downed pilot', the Houthis failed to provide any kind of evidence for their claim except for a drop tank from a RSAF F-15, and the wreckage of an AIM-9M. While officials in Riyadh dismissed this claim, it seems that one of RSAF's vaunted Eagles was at least forced to jettison most of its ordnance in emergency.

Later during the day, the Saudi-led coalition hit back in force by bombing Houthi/Salleh concentrations in Hajjah, Dhamar, Ataq, Aden and Khormaksar, arms depots in Ghula (in Omran province, north of Sana'a), and weapons storage facilities and the Supreme Military Academy in Sana'a.

The Houthi authorities in Sana'a claimed the downing of another 'Saudi aircraft', on 24 May, this time over Sa'ada. As so often, no evidence was provided: on the contrary, such reports only provoked heavy and sustained air strikes on Hudaydah, where Abu Bassam al-Houthi – one of the movement's top LALs – was killed during the bombing of Ja'afari military base.

The Hudaydah area was hit severely on 26 May 2015, when the Saudi-led coalition targeted the local naval base and claimed the destruction of two warships 'operated by Houthis'. Local sources confirmed the sinking of YNS Bilqis, five gunboats and the 'destruction of administrative building' inside the base. Daylami AB and its ammunition depot were the primary targets of air strikes on 28 and 29 May, together with the Houthi camp in the Khawlan District of Sana'a, the main base of the 3rd Presidential Guards Brigade, Presidential Palace, and the main building of the Ministry of Defence on 29 May 2015. Up to 40 additional combat sorties – reportedly resulting in no fewer than 600 'impacts' – hit the Sana'a area on the following day, when the Presidential Palace and the Haj Attan arms depot were hit again, and over 100 killed. Later during the day, bombs of the Saudi-led coalition completely obliterated the historic al-Qahera fort, constructed in the 10th Century and a UNESCO World Heritage Site, on a hill above Yemeni capital.

Air strikes continued targeting the Sana'a area through June 2015: on 5th of that month, the High Command of the Yemeni Army was destroyed – together with five apartment buildings nearby, killing at least 51 (including 25 military officers and other ranks). Other air strikes hit an arms depot in Nahdain, south of the capital, and a camp for displaced persons outside Hajjah, where 55 civilians were massacred. The main building of the Ministry of Defence and the High Command of the Yemeni Army were completely demolished in the course of air strikes on 8 June. A day later, the Saudi-led coalition obliterated the historic, Ottoman-era al-Owrdhli compound outside the Old City of Sana'a. Following two days of break, Sana'a was bombed again on 10 and 11 June 2015, and at least two bombs destroyed several houses in the 2,500-year old Old City, killing at least 50 people, on 12 June 2015.

Technicians of the RSAF, installing GBU-49 laser-homing bombs on an F-15S before the next combat sortie over Yemen. (Ministry of Defence of Saudi Arabia)

An Airbus A440 MRTT in-flight refuelling an E-3 Sentry of the RSAF, during combat operations over Yemen. (RSAF)

Another view of an A440 MRTT, this time during in-flight refuelling of an UAEAF F-16E. (Fahd Rihan, via Mohammed Khalid)

A Kuwaiti F/A-18C (foreground) and an F-15C of the RSAF seen shortly before take-off from King Khalid AB (Khamis Mushayt) for another sortie over Yemen. (via Mohammed Khalid)

Emirati Landing

Through late May and the first half of June, Dengue fever began spreading through Aden. It hit the Houthis particularly hard and decimated their ranks. The Hirak attempted to exploit this for an attack on the international airport – but this was repulsed on 20 June. Left without choice, the RSAF and the UAEAF then subjected the Houthi-controlled part of the city to five days of air strikes, knocking out most of their remaining heavy weapons – but reportedly killing over 150 civilians, too.

Although the position of forces fighting against the Houthi/ Saleh in the Aden area was stabilized by this time, military commanders of the Saudi-led coalition – and Emiratis in particular – concluded that the situation was far from satisfactory. Not only that AQAP established itself in firm control over several districts of this strategically important port: through May and June nearly half of eastern Yemen came under the control of the Jihadists, who imposed themselves upon the local administrators. Left without a choice, the population tolerated this take-over, but protesting and demonstrations against AQAP were reported as early as 2-6 May, especially once the Jihadists banned one of the local preachers from entering Mukalla. Much smaller and even less welcomed by the locals was Daesh, which deployed its 'Wilayat Hadramawt' Brigade to attack the Yemen Army's base in Tarim and nearby positions of the 2nd Mountain Infantry Brigade – which meanwhile sided with the Houthi/Saleh coalition. The Jihadists abducted 14 Yemeni soldiers and beheaded them on 30 April 2015.

Enraged by such developments, and disappointed by the lack of Saudi action, the Emiratis decided to launch an invasion of southern Yemen. To their aid came the fact that the Houthi leadership made a major mistake when issuing a decree that removed all of Saleh's allies from key government positions, on 1 July 2015. Although this announcement was subsequently withdrawn, it caused its damage in so far that Saleh ordered all of the military units loyal to him to withdraw from Aden. As soon as the units involved were out of the city, remaining Houthi positions collapsed on their own.

Exploiting this opportunity, the UAE quickly landed a full brigade of ground forces – comprising two mechanised battalions equipped with AMX-56 Leclerc MBTs and BMP-3 IFVs, an artillery regiment equipped with South African-made, 155mm G6M1A3 self-propelled howitzers, and a regiment of special forces – in Aden, on 13 July. Supported by the Emiratis, and artillery from several warships of the Saudi-led coalition, the Hirak movement then assaulted Aden International Airport. This was secured by 15 July 2015. However, when the Emiratis attempted an advance into the northern suburbs of Dar Sa'ad and at-Tawahi, the Houthi rear-guard knocked out three of their MRAPs. Tawahi was secured only during second attempt, which was supported by Leclerc MBTs and air strikes, on 20 July.

Up to 2,800 RSLF troops followed in the wake of the Emiratis: they cleared Aden International for flying operations. The first aircraft to land there – on 20 July 2015 – was a C-130H from No. 16 Squadron, RSAF. Minutes after its engines stopped, the Houthis plastered the airport with several volleys of BM-21s – apparently without any effect. The air bridge continued and by 24 July not only that the landings of three Saudi C-130s and an Emirati C-17A were recorded, but the UAEAF deployed four of its AH-64D Apache attack helicopters at Aden International, too.

A forlorn MiG-21bis of the former 90th Aviation Brigade, as seen at Anad AB, after this was secured by Emirati ground forces in early August 2015. (via Mohammed Khalid)

A row of UAEAF AH-64s as seen at Aden IAP in mid-August 2015. (via Mohammed Khalid)

A division (four-ship formation) of GBU-49-armed UAEAF's F-16Es rolling for take-off from Khamis Mushayat AB in summer 2015. (Fahd Rihan, via Mohammed Khalid)

Operation Golden Arrow

Following the successful defence of Aden, Hadi's government announced a 'humanitarian cease-fire' to start on the evening of 26 July 2015. However, explaining it had not been informed about any related agreements, the Saudi-led coalition actually reinforced its aerial offensive. This was even more important because, the Emirati ground forces – supported by Hirak – launched Operation Golden Arrow with an advance in the direction of Anad AB on 25 July.

Their first target was the former HQ of the IV Military District of the Yemeni Army in Sabr. This attack encountered fierce resistance and was stalled for at least a day. Supported by additional air strikes, the Emiratis and the Hirak re-attacked on 26 July and captured the base after a battle in which up to 100 combatants from all involved sides were killed. Only a day later, an air strike of the Saudi-led coalition hit a column of Hirak combatants by mistake, killing 12 and injuring more than 40. Nevertheless, the operation continued at good pace: on 2 August 2015, Anad AB was secured following two days of continued fighting and additional air strikes.

Further advances in the northern direction resulted in the Emiratis, the Hirak, and elements of the former Yemeni Army loyal to Hadi – and now under the command of Major-General Ahmed Saif al-Yafaee – securing Labouza and Zinjibar by 7 August, then the entire Ibb province a day later, and then the Shabwa province by 14 August. For a while at least, it appeared that the Saudi-led coalition might continue its ground operations in the direction of Sana'a, and open a battle for the Yemeni capital in a matter of days. However, obviously seeking to link-up with Saudi-supported forces active north of that area, the Emiratis then re-directed their effort towards the east.

In their rear, most of the Saudi troops in Aden were replaced by contingents from Bahrain and Qatar, which launched an advance from Aden in a western direction, towards Bab al-Mandeb and Abyan. Further reinforcements arrived in Aden during early September in the form of 800 Egyptian troops. In turn, these were replaced by a brigade of the Sudanese Defence Forces – consisting of motorized infantry battalions equipped with BTR-70 APCs – which arrived by ship from Asseb in Eritrea, in October and November 2015. The Sudanese assumed the responsibility for security in Aden.

Battle for Ma'arib

Several Yemen Army units based in Ma'rib area sided with the Houthi/Saleh coalition in March and April 2015, but their bases and the town of Ma'rib subsequently came under repeated attacks by local tribes and AQAP. The Houthi/Saleh coalition took steps to link-up with the army forces in question. On 23 April, a brigade-sized unit of the coalition moved in the direction of the town, provoking a fierce clash with tribal levies that raged for days and left dozens killed. A day later, the tribal forces were reinforced by a contingent of about 300 Yemeni regulars, supported by Saudi special forces. These not only sealed the siege of the Houthi/Saleh garrison of Ma'arib, but also led the first major attack on this town. Launched on 1 May 2015, this received intensive air support: the Saudi-led coalition forces are known to have flown at least 150 combat sorties on this day alone. Nevertheless, the ground attack was beaten back with heavy losses on both sides.

A new attempt was launched only on 6 August 2015, when reports indicated the movement of 'hundreds of Saudi-trained Yemeni troops' from the Wadia border crossing, 'driving dozens of tanks and armoured vehicles' in a southern direction. In a matter of just one week, this advance forced the Houthi/Saleh coalition to abandon most of the Shabwa province, including its capital Ataq. By the end of the month, reports indicated vigorous activity by attack helicopters and the deployment of HIMARS artillery rocket systems operated by the Emirati ground forces against Houthi/Saleh forces in this area, and the approach of a mechanized Bahraini force to Ma'arib.[75]

In the light of Saudi and Bahraini attacks from the north, Emirati attacks from the south – and although causing heavy losses in troops and vehicles to Yemeni Army units loyal to Hadi and to tribal levies – the Houthi/Saleh defences in Ma'rib collapsed by 25 August. The coalition forces converged on the town and quickly turned the nearby airfield originally used by oil companies – known as the Safir airfield – into a forward operating base. Up to eight AH-64 Apache and several other helicopters were forward deployed there, together with at least a battery of Emirati-operated Pantsir-21 (SA-22 Greyhound) short-range SAMs. Despite very strict security measures, this deployment did not escape the attention of the Houthi/Saleh coalition. Early in the morning of 4 September 2015, the Safir airfield was targeted by a single OTR-21. The missile hit the local storage depot, causing a massive conflagration that gutted several AH-64s and dozens of vehicles. The death toll was severe too, and included 45 Emirati, 12 Saudi, 5 Bahraini, and an unknown number of Yemeni soldiers – including Sheikh Mohammed Ibn Rashid am-Maktoum, the Prince of Dubai and a Sandhurst-trained military officer. The strike and heavy loss of coalition troops caused not only a shock in the Emirates, but prompted the UAEAF into air strikes on multiple enemy positions west of Ma'rib and in Bayda area, in Ibb und Sana'a too. Furthermore, the Emirati AH-64s decimated one of the armoured brigades of the Houthi/Saleh coalition, equipped with M60A1s and BMP-2s, deployed for a counterattack on the Ma'rib Dam.[76]

A still from a video released by the Houthi-controlled al-Masirah TV-channel, showing a RSLF AH-64 that was claimed as damaged and forced to land inside Yemen in May 2015. (al-Masirah TV)

The End of Manoeuvring Warfare

Although continuously promising an 'offensive on Sana'a', the Saudi-led coalition remained busy mopping up the Ma'rib area through most of September 2015. Late that month, all offensive operations were stopped. The reason for this decision was that Operation Golden Arrow proved too successful: while destroying most of the Houthi/Saleh forces in central Yemen, it came forward at such a pace that in its rear a power vacuum was created – foremost exploited by AQAP. Although from Aden, Hadi lacked any serious power base in that area, while the advances of the Houthi/Saleh coalition from March and April effectively destroyed most of the military in central and southern Yemen. Similarly, the subsequent spread of AQAP into Aden and southern Yemen neutralized whatever was left of the local civilian authorities and police. In combat against the Houthi/Saleh coalition, militias of the Hirak and the HTC proved far more effective than any of the military units still loyal to Hadi, and their leaders repeatedly refused to operate under the control of generals that sided with the 'legitimate president' (as Hadi was generally described in the Arab media). With the loyalists supported by officials in Riyadh, the HTC by 'private Saudi interest', and the Hirak by the Emiratis, these three Yemeni factions often clashed with each other – and then with AQAP too. Correspondingly, the Saudi-led coalition was left without a choice but to stop all offensive operations for at least six months, in order to enable the recruitment, organization and training of a new, coherent Yemen National Army (YNA), loyal only to Hadi.

The centrepiece of related efforts became Anad AB. Meanwhile garrisoned by the 6th Airborne Brigade and the 64th Special Forces Brigade of the RSLF, and a home for sizeable detachments of RSLF's and UAEAF's combat helicopters, this area became a major training base of the YNA too. Between October 2015 and March 2016, no fewer than eight brigades of the YNA were established, including the 1st, 2nd, 3rd, 4th, 19th, and 22nd Infantry Brigades, and the 14th Armoured Brigade. Simultaneously, the Emiratis launched efforts to establish a Yemeni air corps, through providing training to Yemeni pilots and ground personnel on UAE-owned AT-802 light strike aircraft. The first unit equipped with this type became operational in late October, and began providing CAS to Hadi forces in the Ta'izz and Bayda areas.[77]

As soon as the YNA units were ready, they took over the frontlines in central and southern Yemen, while the Emirati and other foreign contingents were gradually withdrawn towards Aden, where they became involved in the development of multiple infra-structure projects instead.

Border War

In regards of Saudi ground operations, the plan for a military intervention in Yemen originally developed by top military commanders in Riyadh was based on several premises. The first was the decision not to launch a major ground operation into Yemen: Yemenis are renowned as fiercely opposing the presence of foreign troops on their soil and officials in Riyadh feared that this would feed Houthi propaganda. The second was the expectation that the Houthi leadership would bow to a combination of air strikes and minor ground operations, as in 2010. Correspondingly, the Saudis adapted defensive stance along the 1,800-kilometre (1,100 miles) long border.

Although meanwhile clearly demarcated, the border between Saudi Arabia and Yemen – which runs from the Red Sea over extensive mountain chains to the so-called 'Empty Quarter' desert – remained rife with smuggling and illicit activity, just as it had for many years. The terrain included steep mountains scattered with boulders and pitted by gullies and deep, scrubby valleys – an ideal ground for guerrilla warfare. Recognizing such threats, the Saudis launched the construction of what became known as the 'Saudi-Yemen Barrier' – a structure made of concrete-filled pipeline three metres high (10ft) – along a stretch of 75 kilometres, in 2003-2004, but further work was cancelled in face of protests from Sana'a.

Following the intervention of 2009-2010, the Royal Saudi Border Guards were expanded in size and allocated funding to construct a large number of fortified outposts at all dominating peaks along the border, in order to prevent possible infiltrations by the Houthis. Concluding that this 1st line of defence was too thinly occupied and the resulting strongpoints easy to isolate, they further developed the 2nd line. This is consisting of forward bases of the Mountain Brigade RSLF – an entirely new unit established on the basis of experiences from 2009-2010 – several battalions of special forces, and a number of forward operating bases for helicopters and light aviation. The result was that the strongholds held by the Border Guards acted as a trip-wire: in case of any attack on these, intervention forces deployed 20-50 kilometres behind the border were well-positioned to counterattack. Furthermore, all the major RSLF units deployed along the border to Yemen began replacing their obsolete armament with US-made M1 Abrams MBTs and M2 Bradley IFVs. Related measures were not yet all in place when the military intervention in Yemen was launched on 26 March 2015. Work on construction of additional fortified outposts was accelerated, but still incomplete by early May, when the Houthi/Saleh coalition re-directed much of its efforts towards the Saudi border, turning this frontline into one of most critical of this war.

Deployment of Cluster Bomb Units

The first large-scale attacks of the Houthi/Saleh coalition on Saudi border posts began on 1 May 2015. Initially, Riyadh confirmed the loss of three troops killed, but claimed that all the assaults were repulsed. Actually, the Saudis were taken by surprise by the huge mix of conventional and guerrilla units they faced, and then encountered the problem of lacking troops necessary to reinforce their border. Their reaction was limited to counter-strikes by fighter-bombers, attack helicopters and artillery. However, on 7 May 2015, the Houthi/Saleh forces not only deployed Russian-made 220mm BM-27 Uragan multiple rocket launcher systems (MRLS) to hit Najran, and then to mine routes along which the Saudi intervention forces advanced, but also claimed one of the counterattacking AH-64s as shot down. It was in the course of an outright hunt for the BM-27 TELs that the contingent of the Moroccan air force – deployed in Saudi Arabia only two days earlier – suffered a very painful loss. Around 1800hrs local time on 10 May 2015, the F-16C serial number 08-8008 was hit by ground fire while searching for a BM-27 TEL. The aircraft crashed, killing its pilot, Lieutenant Yassine Bahti.[78]

In the aftermath of the first attacks on the Saudi border, reports surfaced indicating extensive use of cluster bomb units (CBUs) – such as the US-made CBU-105s and British-made Hunting BL.755s – by the Saudi-led coalition. Cluster bombs are weapons that release or eject smaller submunitions, usually explosive bomblets designed to kill personnel or destroy vehicles. Other CBUs are designed to destroy runways or roads, or deny their use, or short-cut electric power transmission lines. Because such weapons release many small bomblets over a wide area, but the fusing of the same frequently malfunctions, while other weapons are designated to detonate at a later stage, unexploded bomblets remain extremely dangerous for extended periods of time. In effect, unexploded bomblets function like land mines – the use of which is prohibited for 162 nations that signed the Ottawa Treaty in 1997. In the light of this, the use of CBUs was prohibited too – at least for those nations that ratified the Convention on Cluster Munitions, adopted in Dublin, Ireland, in May 2008, and considered a binding international law since 2010. By 2015, 118 states had joined the Convention.

However, Saudi Arabia and most of its allies have never signed either of the two treaties. Correspondingly, although considered 'illegal' by most of Western countries, deployment of CBUs by the Saudi-led coalition in Yemen was legal for the involved military forces. Officials in Riyadh appeared astounded and unprepared to answer related complaints and inquiries, and explained the

On 4 August 2015, an AH-64 Apache attack helicopter of the RSLF was hit by ground fire and forced to make an emergency landing inside Saudi Arabia. The crew of two came away with light injuries. (Yemeni Internet)

Fin of the Moroccan F-16C shot down by Houthis near Wadi Nashour, in northern Yemen, on 10 May 2015. (Yemeni Internet)

deployment of such weapons as CBU-105s with these being legal because they were sold to Saudi Arabia by the USA. Furthermore, and despite increased pressure from abroad, the Saudi-led coalition continued using CBUs even after – in May 2016 – US officials announced an immediate halt of all transfers of such weapons to the desert kingdom.[79]

Faulty Intelligence and Civilian Casualties

Accusations over the deployment of CBUs came hard on the heels of an increasing number of reports about extensive civilian casualties caused by aerial bombardment. Indeed, separate investigations by the UN, Human Rights Watch (HRW) and Amnesty International (AI) have shown that in the first nine months of the intervention, the Saudi-led coalition violated international humanitarian law no less than 152 times. Amongst others, it targeted 41 residential neighbourhoods, 22 medical facilities, and 10 marketplaces.[80] The area most heavily hit in all of Yemen was the town of Sa'ada. Between 26 March and 19 May, no fewer than 210 bombs impacted built-up areas, destroying and damaging hundreds of buildings. In addition to five markets, an empty school, and a crowded petrol station, one attack killed no fewer than 27 members of the single family, including 17 children. Further air strikes struck targets in densely populated areas of Sa'ana, Hudaydah, Ta'izz, Ibb, Lahj, Daleh, Shabwa, Ma'arib and Aden. Unsurprisingly, as early as14 April 2015, unofficial Yemeni sources citing Houthi/Saleh authorities reported as many as 2,571 civilians killed and 3,897 wounded by air strikes. By early September 2015, the same sources were reporting 4,903 civilians killed (including at least 1,128 children), and nearly 11,300 children injured).[81]

This posed the question of the sources of targeting intelligence used by the Saudi-led coalition. While some of the reports cited extensive use of US-provided intelligence, officials in Washington contradicted themselves: some stressed they did not provide detailed targeting information to the Saudis in Yemen, but only broad intelligence on the area in general. Others confirmed that intelligence collected by surveillance drones and satellites was shared with the Saudis, although this was not meant as an approval for individual targets. It remains unknown whether the Saudi officers that received such intelligence saw the information in question in the same light.

On the contrary, an examination of dozens of reports by Saudis and officials of Hadi's government shows that early during the war most of the targeting intelligence was actually provided by the latter, and that the Saudi and allied officers failed to carefully cross-examine the information they received. Indeed, an unofficial Saudi source stressed, 'Initially, there was far too much reliance on the Yemeni government for intelligence and far too little effort to confirm it'. Such statements were de-facto confirmed by Brigadier-General Samir Haj, the official spokesman for Hadi's military, who confirmed the existence of '...a joint military operations rooms in Aden in Riyad, which work together with the coalition countries to coordinate targets for both air strikes and battle operations on the ground'.[82]

Another issue was the deployment of oversized weapons to destroy specific targets: for example, 1000kg LGBs or GPS-assisted bombs were regularly deployed to destroy relatively small houses in the middle of residential areas. This issue was related to the lack of their own reconnaissance platforms, but also the way the RSAF organized the related campaign. Before the war, the Saudis invested heavily into bolstering their intelligence collection capability. All the KE-3As were reconfigured to the RC-135W similar standard; F-15S' were equipped with Goodrich DB-110 reconnaissance pods that had the capability to transfer collected intelligence to their home-base in real time; and Tornado IDS' had received reconnaissance pods. Furthermore, the RSAF obtained a sizeable fleet of simple to use Beech King Air light aircraft, equipped with a wide diversity of sensors.[83] However, due to their limited endurance none of the aircraft in question provided them and their allies with the means to monitor developments on the ground in Yemen 24 hours a day. Correspondingly, the Saudis reacted with intensive reconnaissance operations in order to keep periods without coverage as short as possible.

Moreover, in order to be able to react to any reports about emerging targets on the shortest possible notice, the RSAF began stacking its fighter-bombers into holding patterns over three and then four major battlefields in northern and southern Yemen. Up to a dozen combat-support aircraft – including reconnaissance assets and tankers – and up to 30 combat aircraft, all controlled by E-3 Sentry AWACS, were kept on station at any time of the day, from where they would be ordered into action as necessary. Such operations not only quickly overextended the Saudi fleet of aerial tankers: at the time the war began, the RSAF had too few of its own tankers. Unsurprisingly, Riyadh requested and received support from the USA, in the form of USAF Boeing KC-135s for aerial refuelling operations, starting with 8 April 2015.[84] Foremost, such an organization of combat operations over Yemen resulted in multiple cases where combat aircraft were ordered into action although armed with unsuitable weapons.

Another cause of civilian casualties was the combination of the fact that the Houthis and their allies made extensive use of hospitals and schools to hide their troop concentrations, and regularly declared nearly all of their casualties caused by bombing as 'civilians'. The Saudi -led coalition made regular air strikes on the Yemeni infrastructure, obviously intended to disorganize the authorities of the Houthi/Saleh coalition. Correspondingly, dozens of bridges, gas stations, residential buildings, but also schools, hospitals, factories and minor mosques were bombed out. As the number of such attacks mounted, even those who cheered the Saudi intervention against the Houthi/Saleh coalition early on, began appealing for its end. Only days after Operation Decisive Storm was launched, head of the Justice and Peace Party and Hadi's chief supporter Abdulaziz Jubari publicly stated that the toll on civilians and Yemen's infrastructure was too high.[85]

Public indifference and unaccountability, combined with ignorance of such requests for most of 2015, resulted in a number of often unexplainable mistakes. On 6 July 2015, more than 100 civilians were killed during an air strike on the headquarters of Saleh's GPC party in Sana'a. Only a day later, air strikes on the major base of the 23rd Armoured Brigade in al-Abr, in Hadramawt, not only left more than 30 Yemeni soldiers loyal to Hadi killed, but also helped AQAP overrun this unit and its major base. On 11 July 2015, the Military Hospital in Sana'a was completely demolished, killing scores – including nine children. Other objects targeted on the same day included the residence of Hafez al-Khulani (a prominent supporter of the Houthis), the Yemen Heritage Centre in Aden, the Wedding Hall in Sana'a, and a cement factory outside the capital – which was one of the major foreign investments into the Yemeni economy of recent years. On 28 September 2015, an air strike first struck a pavilion for female guests at the wedding in Wagha village, in the Mocha area, and then the separate pavilion for male guests, killing at least 135. Just a few days later, on 8 October 2015, another wedding party was hit in Sanban, Dhamar province, killing 23.[86]

The most controversial air strike took place on 8 September 2016, when the Saudi-led coalition targeted a funeral ceremony in Sana'a, reportedly killing 140 and wounding 525. Amid fierce accusations of war crimes and reports about massive casualties amongst women and children, it transpired the coalition had bombed the funeral for Ali ar-Rawishan, the father of the interior minister Galal ar-Rawishan – and killed or injured scores of top military and para-military commanders of the Houthi/Saleh coalition. Amongst these were 12 Major-Generals (6 killed) including former chiefs of the military intelligence, former commanders of the VI and VII Military Districts, the Republican Guards, and of three brigades; 7 Brigadier-Generals (all 7 killed), including the minister of interior of the Houthi/Saleh coalition, commander of CSS in Sana'a and two brigade commanders; 6 Colonels (4 killed), 12 other military officers, and 25 top civilian officials. In other words: while certainly targeting a gathering of 'civilian' nature, and very likely causing lots of so-called 'collateral damage', this air strike delivered a major blow against the top ranks of the Houthi/Saleh command structure in the Sana'a area.

Under immense international pressure, and on advice from US officials, the government in Riyadh issued an apology. Subsequently, it launched a process of lessening the dependence on targeting intelligence provided by its Yemeni allies. Proving far from 'perfect', and advancing only step-by-step, this process included US military lawyers providing advice to their Saudi counterparts in how to ensure the legality of air strikes. Furthermore, the RSAF received US software designed to help determine whether certain munitions might cause destruction beyond the target. When this failed to show immediate effects, in May 2016 US officials announced an immediate halt of all transfers of CBUs to Saudi Arabia – indirectly confirming deliveries of such weapons.[87]

Meanwhile, ever louder critique in the media forced the Saudis to re-introduce the practice of deploying their own special forces operators deep inside Yemen and equipping these with mini-UAVs for reconnaissance purposes. Moreover, they began deploying Chinese made, medium-altitude, long-endurance unmanned aircraft systems (MALE UAS) – or UAVs. The resulting combination of new equipment and old methods of intelligence gathering gradually decreased civilian casualties. However, mistakes continue to happen until the present – usually with tragic consequences for Yemeni civilians.[88]

Deaths of Saudi Generals

On 18 May 2015, three waves including up to 20 fighter-bombers targeted all known and suspected command and control centres, communication hubs, and at least one factory for production of IEDs in the Sa'ada area. In revenge, two days later special forces of the Houthi/Saleh coalition overran a Saudi border post south of Najran. In the course of this operation they claimed the destruction of at least two armoured vehicles, to have killed 18 men and shot down another AH-64.[89]

Officials in Riyadh either ignored or denied nearly all of the claims, but there was little doubt that the Saudis were forced to evacuate dozens of villages and close the airport of Najran. The situation worsened significantly on 22 May, when a sizeable concentration of Houthi/Saleh forces attacked the Haradh border crossing, causing lots of damage and casualties. Three days later, they began firing '75km rockets' against targets inside Saudi Arabia, and – on 26 May – the Houthi/Saleh authorities announced their first attack with ballistic missiles at Khamis Mushayt AB.

Furthermore, clearly seeking for an opportunity to hit back, the RSAF then flew particularly fierce air strikes on all bases of the Yemeni special forces in the Sana'a area on 27 May. According to an anonymous local source, just one of the compounds in question was hit by 18 bombs in a matter of two minutes. Over 40 combatants of the Houthi/Saleh coalition were reportedly killed. Almost simultaneously, the Medical School in Hudaydah was completely destroyed too – right at the time the employees gathered to collect their salaries.[90]

Following a week during which it re-deployed additional units and supplies towards the border, the Houthi/Saleh coalition opened another offensive on Saudi Arabia on 5 June 2015. Within the following 48 hours, it claimed to have fired 20 ballistic missiles, including two at Khamis Mushayt AB. According to Saudi sources, one of these was intercepted by MIM-104 Patriot SAMs, in the early hours of that day. Such strikes were followed by a series of attacks by Yemeni special forces: using motorcycle-mounted teams armed with RPG-7s, and ATGMs, these knocked out two AMX-30 MBTs at Jebel Dukhan and six other vehicles at Jebel Atwaliq during the following 24 hours. By 7 June, the Houthi/Saleh coalition claimed to have launched 28 ballistic missiles at Saudi Arabia and – on 10 June – reported that one of its attacks on Khamis Mushayt AB killed the Commander-in-Chief of the RSAF, Lieutenant-General ash-Shaalan. Riyadh promptly countered with an official statement according to which Shaalan died of a heart attack in London. He was replaced by Major-General Abdullah Ibn Ibrahim al-Ghamdi.

The degree to which the Houthi/Saleh coalition was in possession of the initiative in northern Yemen during this period became obvious on 12 June, when its forces defeated a combined tribal and AQAP force in Hazm, capital of the Jawf province, and seized the town. For the rest of the month, attacks on Saudi border posts took place on an almost daily basis. Deploying units of special forces and artillery that sided with it, the Houthi/Saleh coalition made skilful use of rugged terrain to not only overrun isolated outposts or attack nearby villages and minor military bases, but also to launch dramatic incursions up to 30 kilometres inside Saudi Arabia. As well as often ambushing intervening Saudi units, its forces carefully avoided bigger confrontations with the RSLF, and always left huge numbers of mines and improvised explosive devices behind, causing additional losses.

Avoiding all means of detection used by the Saudis and allies, on 21 and 22 June 2015, the Yemenis fired more than 70 rockets at Najran and the nearby airport, and knocked out at least two

M60 MBTs. Four days later, over 200 rockets from BM-21 and BM-27 MRLs hit the al-Mathab military base outside Jizan and ad-Doud military base outside Najran, while another 56 rockets were fired at the al-Qa'am military base in the Zahran area, and Saudi positions at Jebel Dukhan. Although the exact extent of the damage caused by these attacks remains unknown, Saudi authorities subsequently confirmed they had been forced to evacuate most of the local population.[91]

On 29 June 2015, the Houthi/Saleh coalition claimed to have launched three ballistic missiles at the RSAF's GCI station at as-Sail (near Wadi ad-Dwasir), and at the as-Sulayyil and as-Salsabil missile bases. While there is a strong doubt that the Yemenis had any kind of weapons that could reach such distant targets at that point in time, such reports have clearly confirmed that military leaders in Sana'a were in possession of relatively good intelligence about sensitive spots in Saudi Arabia. Furthermore, it has shown that they were at least interested in striking at the Saudi military, even if not in a perfect position to actually do so.

A new round of attacks on the Saudi border was launched on 19 August: the Houthi/Saleh coalition subsequently claimed to have reached the suburbs of Najran, and then to have fired at least one OTR-21 ballistic missile at one of the military bases in this area. During further operations in this area, the Yemenis claimed to have killed Major-General Abdul Rahman Abu Jarfahash Shahani, commander of the 18th Brigade RSLF, and then to have shot down an AH-64 Apache helicopter. Surprisingly enough, this time officials in Riyadh confirmed at least the latter loss, although the reason stated was the same as usual: 'technical malfunction'.[92]

Jizan Front

The Houthi/Saleh campaign of attacks on the Saudi border reached its high point during the second half of September 2015, by when the involved forces were applying well-tested tactics. Usually, they would first deploy teams equipped with anti-tank guided missiles (ATGMs) – like Russian-made 9M113 Konkurs, 9M133 Kornet-E and a few US-made BGM-71 TOW – to take out specific vehicles or bunkers. The BM-21s and BM-27s would then target nearest military bases, and sew mines along routes leading in the direction of the border. Meanwhile, special forces would start assaulting the border outposts, while motorcycle-mounted teams armed with RPG-7s and US-made BGM-47 Dragons would infiltrate into Saudi rear. Columns of RSLF intervention forces would thus drive into unknown minefields, or rush into ambushes at places not directly hit by the fighting. Some raiding parties deployed into Saudi Arabia were armed with man-portable air defence systems (MANPADs), but deployment of M167 Vulcan towed anti-aircraft cannons was noted too. Although exact details the effectiveness of either remain evasive, it transpires that during the first year of this war they at least managed to damage numerous attack helicopters of the RSLF and the RSNG, and thus forced their crews to keep their distance. During the final phase of any such operation, the Yemenis would plaster the Saudi intervention forces with BM-21s and BM-27s again, in order to pin them down while the raiding party was exfiltrated.

Operating in this fashion, the Houthi/Saleh coalition achieved an entire series of successes in areas near Jizan and Najran, between 19 and 27 September 2015, knocking out two dozen armoured vehicles (including at least one M1A2S Abrams MBT, a number of M2A2 Bradleys and dozens of other armoured vehicles), and killing Brigadier-General Ibrahim Hamzi, the deputy commander of the 8th Brigade RSLF.[93]

The situation along the Saudi border began to change during mid-October 2015, when the RSLF – with help of improved reconnaissance – began deploying its special forces to intercept and track down enemy raiding parties inside Yemen. In one of the first such operations, a group of Yemeni special forces was completely destroyed near al-Khoba, in the Jizan area, on 15 October.[94]

Saudi Scud Hunt

As described earlier, following two nights of severe air strikes on the bases of the MBG in and around Sa'ana on 28 and 29 March 2015, the Saudi-led coalition declared most of the Yemeni stocks of ballistic missiles as neutralized. This claim proved premature, and another round of air strikes on bases of the MBG was flown starting with 21 April 2015: tragically, this time either several bombs missed their targets, or the ensuing conflagration caused the deaths of up to 46 and severe injuries to more than 250 civilians.[95]

As time was to show, dozens of missiles and several TELs of the MBG survived this onslaught: indeed, the Yemeni personnel exploited the cease-fire of 12-15 May 2015 to extract surviving equipment from the demolished bases and return it to business. Unsurprisingly, a video surfaced depicting a single 9P117M TEL underway in the Amran Governorate, north of Sana'a, during this period. This was the first trace of evidence that at least some of the MBG's heavy equipment survived the Saudi-led aerial onslaught. The first strikes with ballistic missiles against Saudi Arabia were reported by the Iranian media late that month.[96] However, these saw the deployment of BM-27s and such do-it-yourself weapons as the M-75 – whose designation is apparently based on its range of 75 kilometres (47 miles). When multiple BM-27 TELs were knocked out by air strikes, the Houthi/Saleh coalition began to improvise: intact launch tubes were recovered and installed on commercial trucks instead. Correspondingly, their rocket attacks on Saudi strongpoints, military bases and villages continued almost without disruption.

Following a night of particularly intensive air strikes on Sana'a, the Houthi/Saleh coalition ordered the first ballistic missile attack on Saudi Arabia, at 02.45hrs in the morning of 6 June 2015. Reportedly, the R-17E – fired from an unknown area somewhere along the western part of the Saudi-Yemeni border – was intercepted by two Saudi-operated MIM-104 Patriot SAMs short of its target – Khamis Mushayt. Patriots were to play a decisive role in the defence of Saudi Arabia over the following weeks and months because by 30 July the Houthi/Saleh reportedly fired up to 20 SS-1 and Hwasong-6 missiles at Saudi Arabia. Nearly 40% of these were claimed as shot down, while most of the others appear to have failed after launch or entirely missed their target.[97]

On 26 August, the Houthi/Saleh coalition fired a single R-17E from the Sana'a area at Jizan in Saudi Arabia. The roar of the launch was heard in many parts of Sana'a – but so was that of its interception: the Scud was shot down by a US-made MIM-104 Patriot-2 (PAC-2) SAM, about 30km short of its target. Riyadh not only confirmed the shoot-down, but also claimed the TEL in question to have been destroyed in an air strike a few minutes later.[98]

Although claiming the interception and downing of every single R-17E and OTR-21 fired into Saudi Arabia, Riyadh staged an outright 'Scud Hunt' in Yemen during the summer of 2015. Deploying not only its EK-3As and Beech King Airs, equipped with a wide array of electronic and optical sensors, but also F-15S' and Tornado IDS' for this purpose in hundreds of reconnaissance sorties, the Saudis proved reasonably effective in this regard – especially considering the rugged terrain of Yemen. Namely, they tracked down and scored their first 'confirmed kill' against one of the Yemeni-operated TELs – an OTR-21 launcher – on or around 1 September 2015. With this, related efforts of the Saudi-led coalition proved 100% more effective than those run by the US-coalition in Iraq of January and February 1991: namely, during the II Gulf War, the USA and allies failed to knock out even one Iraqi TEL, despite often flying up to 400 related reconnaissance and combat sorties a day.

During the late summer and early autumn of 2015, the number of ballistic missile attacks by the Houthi/Saleh-coalition continued to increase. Indeed, such attacks achieved some of the biggest successes for this side in the conflict to date. As described above, on 4 September a single OTR-21 strike against Safir airfield near Ma'rib delivered the biggest single blow upon the Saudi-led coalition so far. Another blow of similar importance might have been delivered against Khamis Mushayt AB, on 15 October 2015, when a single R-17 (fired from within the compound of the Presidential Palace in Sana'a) reportedly scored a direct hit.[99]

In December 2015, the Houthi/Saleh-coalition announced the introduction into service of two 'new' weapons to its arsenal – in the form of missiles named the Qahir-1 and, a few weeks later, Qahir-2M. Both of these were little other than obsolete S-75 Dvina (SA-2 Guideline) SAMs. Furthermore, in early 2016, the Missile Force announced that it had repaired one of the SA-2 SAM-sites, and published a video showing it in operation. On 20 January, the Houthi-controlled media claimed a 'Saudi F-15' as shot down. The video released in support of this claim showed wreckage of an UAV. In turn, reports in the Saudi social media indicate that this SA-2 site was tracked down and destroyed by the RSAF.

As described in Volume 1, Yemen obtained a total of 964 V-755 missiles for the SA-2 systems in the 1970s. Large numbers of these remained available – if not necessarily in operational condition – by the time most of them were taken over by the Houthi/Saleh coalition. The S-75 had a limited surface-to-surface capability against targets with a large radar cross section, and was deployed for such purposes in multiple conflicts between 1973 and 1995. Correspondingly, engineers and other technical personnel of the former YAF had more than enough know-how, opportunity, and material to repair some of the radars, and at least one launcher for use in surface-to-air mode, and then to develop their own surface-to-surface variant – deployable without radar support. While lacking the range, precision, and the punch of dedicated designs, conversion of S-75s to Qahir-1 and Qahir-2M was foremost important because it provided the Houthi/Saleh with a relatively large number of surface-to-surface missiles with reasonable range.

The Saudis, followed by the Emiratis, reacted promptly to the emergence of this new threat – by deployment of Chinese-made Chengdu Pterodactyl I (exported under the designation CH-4 Wing Loong) UAVs for reconnaissance over Yemen. Generally similar in capabilities, equipment, and performance to the well-known General Atomics MQ-1/RQ-1 Predator – which Washington refused to sell to the two countries – the Wing Loongs vastly expanded the reconnaissance and intelligence-gathering capabilities of the RSAF and the UAEAF. Indeed, it seems that these UAVs were crucial for the interception and destruction of another OTR-21 TEL operated by the Houthi/Saleh coalition, somewhere north of Sana'a, on 1 January 2016, only minutes after this fired a missile in the direction of Jizan. Whether the TEL in question was attacked and destroyed by one of the UAVs too, remains unknown. What is certain is only that Saudi Arabia (which placed its first order for CH-4s back in 2011) and the United Arab Emirates (which placed its order in 2014), operate variants of this system that can deploy such Chinese made guided weapons as the BA-7 air-to-ground missile, YZ-212 laser-homing bomb, YZ-102A anti-personnel bomb, and LS-6 miniature guided bomb.[100]

The Saudis achieved a similar success in January 2018, when – following a series of seven launches of Qahir-2Ms at Saudi Arabia and allied positions in the Ma'rib area – their air force tracked down and destroyed another of the TELs operated by the Missile Force.

Early during their campaign against the Saudi border, forces of the Houthi/Saleh coalition still had the freedom to launch frequent attacks with BM-21 MRLS'. This photograph shows such an attack in Najran area, in June 2015. (al-Masirah TV)

A snap-shot showing the contrail left by an OTR-21 that failed upon launch from the Nuqum area of Sana'a in the summer of 2015. (Yemeni Internet)

A still from a video released by al-Masirah TV in October 2015, showing a 9M714 TEL operated by the Houthi/Saleh coalition, with an OTR-21 Tochka (SS-21 Scarab) ballistic missile about to be fired. (al-Masirah TV)

Wreckage of the first 9M714 TEL operated by the Houthi/Saleh coalition that was tracked down and destroyed by the Saudi-led coalition. (al-Masirah TV)

A Saudi MIM-104 gunner that shot down a Qaher-1 ballistic missile fired in the direction of Najran in December 2015. (via T. S.)

The second 9M714 TEL operated by the Houthi/Saleh coalition that was tracked down and destroyed by the Saudi-led air power in mid-October 2015. (via T. S.)

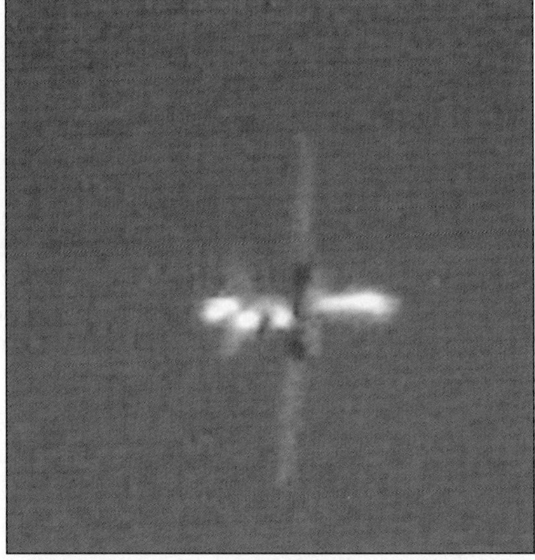

A CH-4 Wing Loong (Pterodactyl I) UCAV as seen high above Sana'a in October 2015. (Photo by Wadhah al-Ganad)

CHAPTER 6
STALEMATE

Having secured Aden and Ma'rib, and while busy working-up the YNA, the Saudi-led coalition turned its attention to three other neuralgic fronts: the western-most section of the Saudi-Yemeni border; the besieged city of Ta'izz; and the issue of securing the ports of Bab al-Mandeb and Mocha, on the Yemeni coast of the Red Sea. Continuous, UN-sponsored peace-negotiations in Kuwait, extremely problematic terrain, amd also the cessation of all offensive operations starting with September 2015, offered the Houthi/Saleh coalition plenty of time to heavily mine all of the approach routes and fortify their positions. Combined with the ever increasing deployment of YNA forces instead of foreign contingents, this resulted in the war entering its next phase: one in which the tempo of combat operations was significantly decreased, and which is lasts until today.

Siege of Ta'izz

Ta'izz, the historic centre of political opposition to Sana'a – and so also the Hadi's, and then to Houthi/Saleh's governments, too – meanwhile developed into the scene of one of the most bitterly fought battles of this war. Although the Houthis and allied military units that sided with Saleh encountered little resistance in the city early on, various local parties exploited the weak presence of their opponents to gradually build-up. Initially, the resistance to the Houthi/Saleh coalition was centred around the remnants of the 35th Armoured Brigade. This was reinforced by a tribal militia of Sheikh Hammoud al-MIkhlafi – former officer of the Political Security Branch, affiliated with the Islah Party, and an ally of Major-General Ali Mohsen. While often wrongly described as 'fighting for Hadi', none of the armed groups in question ever pledged allegiance to the exiled president, and – with few exceptions – they generally received next to no support from the outside. Furthermore, the composition of the forces in question changed over time: while the militias at least associated with the Islah Party used to play a dominant role early on, they were gradually superseded by the Quietists, who proved far better organized and a much more effective fighting force. Ironically, they were often misdeclared as 'AQAP' by both the Houthi/Saleh and the Western media alike.

Street fighting and artillery exchanges began to rage through Ta'izz in late April 2015, prompting the Houthi/Saleh coalition to reinforce its local units. These meanwhile consisted of roughly half of the 35th Armoured Brigade, but also most of the 22nd Armoured Brigade, some special forces of the Yemeni Army, and numerous contingents of Houthi militias. The first large clash took place on 20 May, when the militias secured the Jabal al-Arous military base and the Jebel Sabir, provoking the Houthi/Saleh coalition to subject the city to indiscriminate, days-long artillery barrages that killed dozens of civilians. Five days later, the Islah Party's militias – supported by Saudi air strikes – secured the base of the 35th Armoured Brigade.

As the developments on other frontlines forced the Houthi/Saleh coalition to withdraw some of their forces from the second-largest city in Yemen, the Islah and the Quietists launched another attack, and secured the HQ of the Security Directorate on 16 August 2015. Once again, the reaction was for the Houthi/Saleh forces to plaster the Old City and the captured base with artillery. Shelling continued for days longer: busy elsewhere, and uncertain about the exact positions of multiple parties meanwhile involved in this battle, the Saudi-led coalition was reluctant to target anything. Whenever it tried to do so, it caused extensive civilian casualties. For example, on 20 August 2015, not only were 23 civilians were killed by artillery shelling, but bombs of the Saudi-led coalition killed more than 50.[101]

By October 2015, the Houthi/Saleh coalition's control of the city was limited to the centre and all the main roads leading out of the city, while local militias controlled most of the outskirts. The influence of the local branch of the Islah party greatly diminished following an air strike that hit one of its camps in Ta'izz, on 17 October, when 30 were killed and 40 injured. During the following weeks, the besieged defenders began receiving CAS from fighter-bombers of the Saudi-led coalition forward deployed at Anad AB, but also in the form of para-dropped supplies and arms. Furthermore, four IOMAX AT-802s – all donated by the UAE – of the newly-established Yemeni Air Corps became operational over Ta'izz. However, a para-dropped parcel containing anti-tank missiles dropped over Ta'izz on 29 October detonated on landing, while the Houthis claimed to have shot down one of the transport aircraft involved. Air strikes on positions of the Houthi/Saleh coalition in the Ta'izz area began in earnest on 1 December 2015, when up to 30 sorties were reported – as was massive collateral damage, including 70 civilians killed and injured.

Ta'izz remained the target of 20-30 air strikes a day through most of the following three months, until the siege was finally broken on 11 March 2016. The operation in question was initiated by the 22nd Brigade YNA, which punched through the Houthi positions on the western side of the city, while tribal militias assaulted those in the east, thus opening the way for mechanised formations of the Saudis and allies. After losing the main base of the 35th Armoured Brigade, resistance from the Houthi/Saleh forces collapsed, and they rapidly withdrew towards the north-eastern suburbs and the local airport. Even then, the fighting for this city continued well into November 2016, when a renewed offensive of the YNA – supported by plentiful of air strikes and helicopter gunships – finally forced combatants of the Houthi/Saleh coalition away from Ta'izz.

As well as combat helicopters, in October 2015 the Emiratis deployed at least four IOMAX AT-802 light striker aircraft to Anad AB, in southern Yemen. This example was photographed while rolling for take-off, armed with GBU-49 laser-homing bombs. The aircraft are flown by combined, Emirati and Yemeni crews. (Pit Weinert Collection)

Since May 2015, RSAF F-15S' are increasingly deployed for providing CAS to ground forces. This example from No. 6 Squadron was photographed while underway over northern Yemen, armed with no fewer than 10 Mk.82 general-purpose bombs, two AGM-65 Maverick air-to-ground missiles, and the usual combination of AIM-9M and AIM-120 air-to-air missiles. (Fahd Rihan, via Mohammed Khalid)

An AS.532 Cougar helicopter from No. 99 Squadron, seen while in-flight refuelling from a KC-130H of No. 32 Squadron, RSAF. Much less glamorous than fighter-bombers, these helicopters have a vital role in deploying Saudi special forces behind enemy lines, and also in serving as combat search and rescue platforms. (Fahd Rihan, via Mohammed Khalid)

Armed with Diehl BGT Defence IRIS-T air-to-air missiles, this EF-2000 was photographed while taking off for a combat air patrol over Yemen in early 2017. (Fahd Rihan, via Mohammed Khalid)

Bab al-Mandeb and Beyond

On 22 September 2015, a combined Emirati, Bahraini, Qatari, Sudanese and YNA ground force – supported by a mercenary force consisting of Australians and Colombians, Mirage 2000s of the QEAF and Su-24s of the Sudanese Air Force – launched an advance from Aden in a western direction, towards Bab al-Mandeb, but with one prong going for Ta'izz. Simultaneously, Saudi, Egyptian and Emirati forces attacked several of the Yemen-owned islands in the Red Sea, with plentiful aerial support.[102] Initially proceeding at a very good pace, this operation resulted in the capture of Bab al-Mandeb, in early October 2015. However, the coalition's subsequent advance further north was stalled when a disgruntled YNA soldier assassinated RSLF Colonel Abdullah as-Sahyan and Emirati Colonel Sultan al-Ketbi, at the forward headquarters near Sha'ab al-Jenn, outside Bab al-Mandeb on 14 December 2015. Said to have been one of most competent Saudi commanders – and claimed by the Houthi/Saleh as killed in an attack by a ballistic missile that had killed 'dozens of mercenaries' – Sahyan appears to have been a crucial commander involved in the offensives on Bab al-Mandeb and Ta'izz. Certainly enough, his early demise was badly felt by the Saudi-led coalition.[103]

The fighting experienced new qualities of intensity during the following weeks, especially after the failed, UN-sponsored, cease-fire announced for 18 December 2015. On that, and during the following days, the Houthi/Saleh coalition fired up to a dozen ballistic missiles at targets in Saudi Arabia, in the Ma'rib and the Bab al-Mandeb area. Despite ever higher claims about casualties supposedly caused by these, most of the missiles either failed after launch or were shot down by air defences, which were meanwhile reinforced by Saudi-operated PAC-3 SAMs.[104]

On the contrary, the Saudi-led coalition then launched not only over 1,200 combat sorties within three days, but also unleashed two brigades of the YNA supported by Bahraini mechanized infantry, and self-propelled artillery of Kuwaiti ground forces, from south-western Saudi Arabia into an attack on Haradh and Hazm in the Jouf province. This assault obviously took the Houthi/Saleh coalition by surprise, the YNA units then quickly advanced nearly 35 kilometres deep inside Yemen. On their left flank, Saudi special forces reportedly found and destroyed dozens of tunnels used by the Yemenis to infiltrate Saudi Arabia. On 20 December 2015, Saudi paratroopers were airdropped into the Nihm district of eastern Sana'a, enabling the YNA and several local militias to launch an advance along the road from Ma'rib. A day later, the allies thus took the Republican Guard base at Bayt Dahrah, barely 20 kilometres outside Sana'a. With this, even the Daylami AB came within artillery range of the Saudi-led coalition.

In early January 2016, Saudi Marines and YNA troops landed at the port of Midi, in Hajjah province. After repelling several counterattacks by the quantitatively superior forces of the Houthi/Saleh coalition, the troops then launched a slow but systematic advance towards the town of Hajjah. Meanwhile, the Saudi special forces raided several Houthi training camps in the Sa'ada province. After building up their stocks of supplies, the Saudis pushed inland later the same month and almost reached the town of Hajjah before being stopped by minefields, protected by extensive fortifications. All of the operations in question received plentiful air support: Emirati and Saudi AH-64s were extremely

Operations against forces of the Houthi/Saleh coalition in the Bab al-Mandeb area saw the significant involvement of Mirage 2000 fighter-bombers of the Qatar Emiri Air Force – like this example, photographed in 2011 during operations in Libya. (USN photo)

Kuwaiti F/A-18Cs also flew air strikes in support of operations in the Bab al-Mandeb area. This example was photographed while landing at King Khalid AB, outside Khamis Mushayt, in July 2017. (Ahmed Hader, via Mohammed Khalid)

active in rocketing enemy ground positions and knocking out whatever armour the Houthi/Saleh coalition managed to bring to the frontlines, while fighter-bombers primarily targeted roads in the Sana'a area.

On 24 February 2016, local militia supported by Saudi and Emirati air strikes defeated the counter-attack of two brigades of the Houthi/Saleh coalition and then launched an attack that ended with the capture of the main base of the 312th Armoured Brigade in Fardhat Nihm after a two-week long siege. Also, on 24 February, the YNA – all of which was now officially under the command of Major-General Ali Mohsen al-Ahmar, appointed as Hadi's Minister of Defence despite fierce protests from many of groups fighting against the Houthi/Saleh coalition – took the Camp Arqoob, a large military base 40 kilometres south-east of Sana'a. Reportedly, this prompted most of the troops of one of the four Presidential Guard brigades to defect to the Saudi-led side.

In mid-April 2016, the Emirati ground forces, in cooperation with the YNA and militias of what was now the Hadramawt Council (HC; former Hadramawt Tribal Council), launched a rapid advance from Aden in the direction of Zinjibar. Days later, on 24 April 2016, the Emiratis launched an amphibious landing in Mukalla, a major port in southern Yemen, held by AQAP since autumn 2015. Simultaneously, HC forces launched an advance from the mountains north of the town in three directions towards the south, supported by a few Mi-8/17 helicopters of the Yemeni Air Corps, and multiple air strikes of the UAEAF. After offering some resistance, the AQAP forces rapidly collapsed: Mukalla and nearby Buwaish were all secured by 26 April 2016.[105]

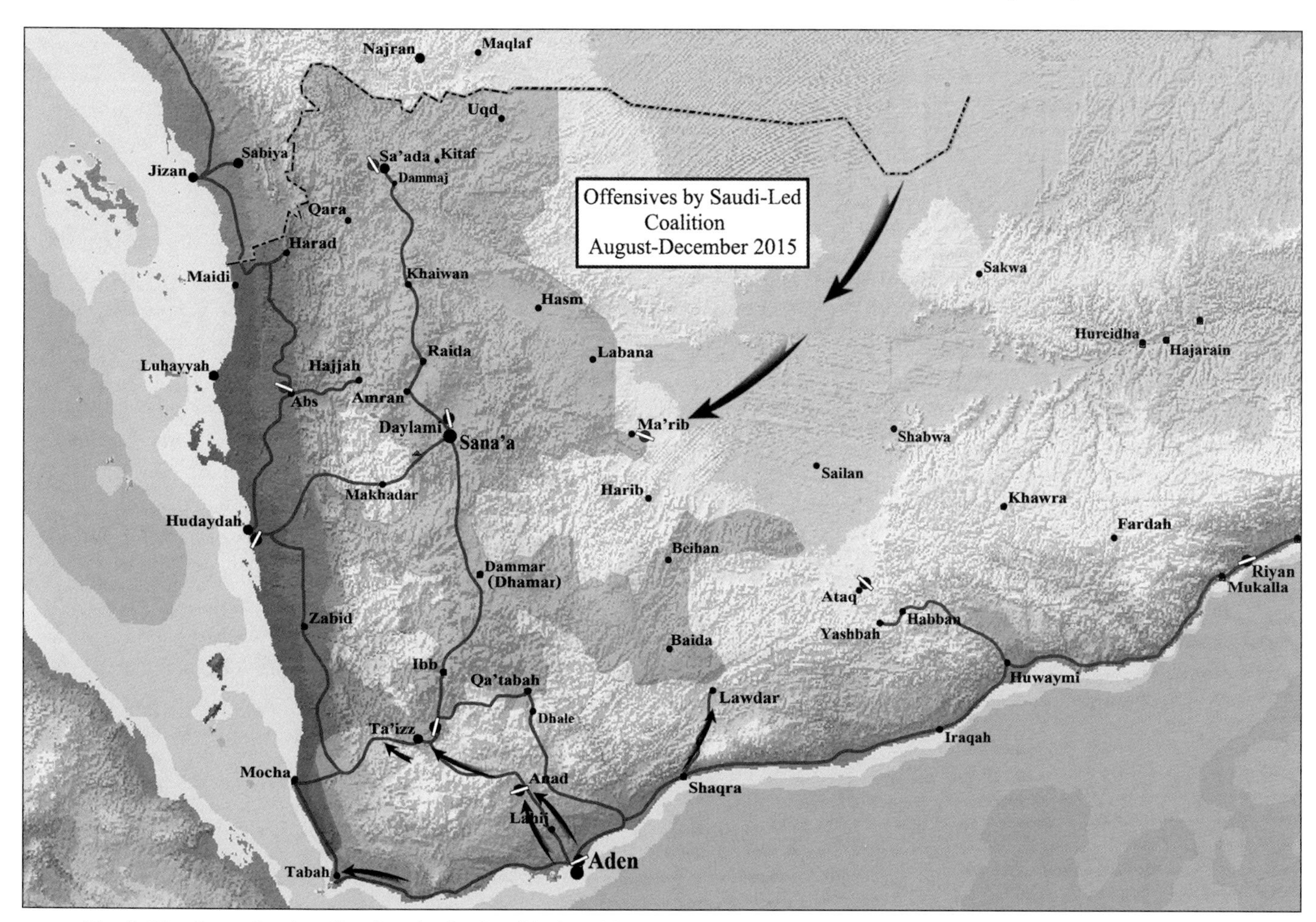

Map 3 Directions of major offensives by the Saudi-led coalition undertaken in period August-December 2015. (Map by Tom Cooper)

A pair of Emirati F-16Es armed with GBU-49 laser-homing bombs, rolling for take off from Khamis Mushayt. (Fahd Rihan, via Mohammed Khalid)

Operated primarily from Asseb air base, in Ertirea, Emirati Mirage 2000s saw intensive deployment in support of combat operations along the Yemeni coast of the Red Sea, starting in late 2015. (USAF photo)

An F-16C of the Egyptian Air Force (recognizable from large parts of its wing pained in orange), releasing a bomb while underway high in the skies over Sana'a, in January 2016. (Yemeni Internet)

Escalation of the Missile War

By mid-2016, the Saudis had claimed the destruction of at least three TELs used by the Houthi/Saleh coalition to fire missiles at Saudi Arabia. However, the longer the war dragged on, the more time was left for missile specialists that defected from Hadi to develop the idea to extend the range of the North Korean-made Hwasong-6 missiles and thus obtain a weapon with which they could hit targets deep inside Saudi Arabia too. The Hwasong-6 was already known as the Extended Range Scud, because it can reach targets 310 miles away – compared to 187 miles for the R-17. This extra reach came at the price of a reduced payload (from 2,200 pounds to just 1,540 pounds). Through an extension project launched by the 'Missile Research and Development Centre' of the Houthi/Saleh coalition, at least six Hwasongs were converted into missiles named Burkan-1. While such an undertaking might appear beyond the abilities of Yemeni engineers, an Iraqi engineer who – back in 1987-1988 – worked on a similar project based on the original, Soviet-manufactured R-17 system, the al-Hussein missile, explained the relative simplicity of the corresponding undertaking as follows:

The R-17E is quite simple. From tip towards the rear, it contains a warhead, then a room for equipment like gyro and timer, then the fuel tank which is about 1.35 metres long, and the oxidizer tank that is about 2.7 metres long. At the rear end is the engine.

Stretching the missile body is no major problem, but stretching fuel tanks is one. The simplest solution – the one we applied early on in Iraq – is to take a tank from another missile, cut its central section and insert it into the tank of the modified missile…Before launching domestic production of stretched fuel tanks, we used tanks from three R-17Es to create one for the al-Hussein missile. The problem is the cutting of that fuel tank: doing that with usually available means results in destruction of the tank. We found an engineer trained in England before 1951. He modified the cutting machine so that the tank was not damaged. Another problem was welding the new, extended fuel tank. We had to use argon for welding. The third problem was the centre of gravity. During early trials, missiles came back down horizontally and slowly, and failed to explode. The solution was to move air pressure cylinders from the rear to the front of the missile, near the warhead, to make its nose heavier. The final problem was that of batteries. Some of missiles fired at Tehran in 1988 failed to detonate for this reason. In April 1988, we installed a second battery, and this never happened again.

After two 'test-firings' of Burkan-1 against Khamis Mushayt, the most spectacular attack was launched on 28 October 2016, when a missile fired in the direction of Mecca – the holiest place in Islam – or Jeddah, was intercepted about 65 kilometres (40 miles) short of its target.

The use of shorter-ranged Qaher-1 and Qaher-2 continued through all of 2016 and well into early 2017 too, forcing the Emiratis to bolster their two Russian-made Pantsir S1 (SA-22 Greyhound) SAM-sites already deployed in Yemen through the addition of at least one MIM-104 Patriot SAM-site. During the first year of its operations in Yemen, the latter site reportedly intercepted 70 ballistic missiles fired in direction of Ma'rib. In November 2016, Saudi Arabia claimed to have shot down 11 ballistic missiles fired from Yemen. Similarly, by April 2017, ground-based Emirati-operated air defences deployed between Mocha and Bab al-Mandeb intercepted a total of 12 SSMs fired by the Houthi/Saleh coalition.[106]

In early 2017, the Houthi/Saleh coalition introduced its next new weapon – the Burkan-2. Sometimes reported as Zelzal-2, this seems to be wearing the same designation as the well-known family of Iranian-made missiles. Actually, Burkan-2s are based on at least five R-17s or Hwasong-6s damaged during air strikes early in the war, and subsequently repaired, while what the Houthis call 'Zelzal-2' proved to be little other than Soviet/Russian-made S-24 heavy unguided 240mm rockets, recovered from ammunition dumps of the former YAF. Burkan-2s show obvious similarities to the classic design of the R-17, but also a much shortened main body, with an entirely new warhead-section of smaller diameter at the front. Their appearance added plenty of fuel to the fire of those claiming that Tehran was 'increasing the pace of arms transfers to the Houthis', although next to no evidence was provided in support of that thesis. On the contrary, of particular interest is that some of the strikes by Burkan/Zelzal-2s were supported by operations of Qasef-1 miniature UAVs, deployed to hit radar systems of Saudi Patriot SAMs.[107]

However, the longer the war went on, the clearer it became that the Houthi/Saleh coalition was exhausting its remaining stocks of missiles. For this reason, but also due to much improved efficiency of the Saudi and Emirati reconnaissance, such attacks were meanwhile launched very rarely. Whenever attempted, the consequence was swift and effective retaliation. For example, late in the evening of 23 September 2017, the RSAF flew a highly successful air strike on a site used to fire missiles at Khamis Mushayt. Reportedly, this not only knocked out another TEL, but left most of the involved launching crew dead. Similarly, when the 'Missile Research and Development Centre' of the Houthi/Saleh coalition hit a school in Jizan with a single Qaher-2M, on 10 October 2017, the Saudis tracked down and destroyed the launcher and the involved team in the Hudaydah area, in a matter of one hour.[108]

Nevertheless, by using spares apparently smuggled in from Iran, the Missile Command intensified its 'Missile War' against Saudi Arabia in November and December of 2017, and January 2018. It repaired and modified at least four R-17Es or Hwasong-6s into the missile designated Burkan-2H. A total of four of these were fired, two of which malfunctioned upon launch. The other two reached the Riyadh area. On 4 November 2017, one fell apart while descending upon Riyadh International: one part of the missile was intercepted by PAC-3s, but the warhead hit empty space close to the runway. The Burkan-2H fired at Riyadh on 19 December was intercepted by Patriots. In January 2018, the Missile Force fired a total of eight Qahir-2Ms, of which two or three were at targets inside Yemen, and the rest in Saudi Arabia: at least two of the missiles fired in the direction of Najran were intercepted by PAC-2s and PAC-3s.

Table 5: Known deployments of SSMs by Houthi/Saleh Coalition, 2015-2017

Date	Missile Type	Target Area	Results
6 June 2015	R-17E	Khamis Mushayt AB	confirmed intercept 30km from target
7 June 2015	R-17E	Khamis Mushayt AB	unclear
10 June 2015	R-17E	Khamis Mushayt AB	unclear
16 Jun 2015	R-17E	Jizan	reportedly intercepted
29 June 2015	R-17E	RSAF GCI station as-Sail, Wadi ad-Dwasir	unclear
29 June 2015	R-17E	As-Sulayyil missile base	unclear
29 June 2015	R-17E	As-Salsabil missile base	unclear
20 Aug 2015	OTR-21	Unknown	unclear
26 Aug 2015	R-17E	Jizan, electricity station	confirmed intercept 30km from target
26 Aug 2015	Qaher-1	Jizan	reportedly intercepted
4 Sep 2015	OTR-21	Safir airfield, Ma'arib	direct hit
10 Sep 2015	OTR-21	Unknown	missile failed upon launch from Nuqum, Sana'a area
11 Oct 2015	R-17E	Khamis Mushayt AB	unclear
15 Oct 2015	R-17E	Khamis Mushayt AB	possible hit; fire and ambulances reported from targeted area
24 Nov 2015	R-17E	Khamis Mushayt AB	reportedly intercepted 30km from target
4 Dec 2015	Qaher-1	Jizan Airport	unclear
9 Dec 2015	Qaher-1	Camp Al-Ain al-Harreh, Jizan	unclear
9 Dec 2015	Qaher-1	Camp as-Saleh, Jizan	unclear

Date	Missile Type	Target Area	Results
11 Dec 2015	Qaher-1	Al-Jamarak	unclear
13 Dec 2015	Qaher-1	Khamis Mushayt AB	possible hit;
18 Dec 2015	Qaher-1	Najran	miss; fell east of town
18 Dec 2015	Qaher-1	Ma'rib	confirmed intercept, 20km from target
19 Dec 2015	Qaher-1	at-Tawwal border crossing, Najran	hit near museum
19 Dec 2015	Qaher-1	Al-Wawal border crossing	Hit
19 Dec 2015	OTR-21	Ma'rib	confirmed intercept, 30km from target
20 Dec 2015	Qaher-1	Khamis Mushayt AB	unclear
21 Dec 2015	Qaher-1	Jizan	confirmed intercept 35km from target
21 Dec 2015	Qaher-1	Jizan airport	confirmed intercept 20km from target
22 Dec 2015	Qaher-1	Aramco Facility, Jizan	confirmed intercept 35km from target
23 Dec 2015	Qaher-1	Khamis Mushayt AB	missed
24 Dec 2015	OTR-21	Zobab, Bab al-Mandeb	confirmed intercept 25km from target
26 Dec 2015	Qaher-1	Najran	confirmed intercept 21km from target
27 Dec 2015	Hwasong-6	Najran	reportedly intercepted
27 Dec 2015	Qaher-1	Jizan	unclear
28 Dec 2015	Qaher-1	Najran	reportedly intercepted
30 Dec 2015	Qaher-1	Aramco Facility, Jizan	reportedly intercepted
31 Dec 2015	Qaher-1		unclear
1 Jan 2016	R-17E or Hwasong-6	Jizan	reportedly intercepted
7 Jan 2016	Qaher-1	Jizan	confirmed intercept 25km from target
17 Jan 2016	OTR-21	Ma'rib	possible hit on Camp Bairaq
18 Jan 2016	OTR-21	Ma'rib	confirmed intercept 35km from target
30 Jan 2016	OTR-21	Anad AB	unclear
8 Feb 2016	R-17E	Khamis Mushayt AB	unclear
8 Feb 2016	Qaher-1	Abha	reportedly intercepted
9 Feb 2016	Qaher-1	Jizan Airport	confirmed intercept 56km from target
13 Feb 2016	Qaher-1	Abha Airport	confirmed intercept 18km from target
3 Mar 2016	OTR-21	Ma'rib	unclear
9 May 2016	R-17E	Khamis Mushayt AB	confirmed intercept 32km from target
9 May 2016	Qaher-1	Abha	confirmed intercept 17km from target
13 May 2016	Qaher-1	Jizan	unclear
20 May 2016	Qaher-1	Jizan	unclear
31 May 2016	Qaher-1		reportedly intercepted
6 Jun 2016	R-17E	Khamis Mushayt AB	confirmed intercept
3 Jul 2016	Qaher-1	Abha	confirmed intercept
23 Jul 2016	Qaher-1	Najran	confirmed intercept
10 Aug 2016	Qaher-1	TBC	confirmed intercept
10 Aug 2016	Qaher-1	TBC	confirmed intercept
16 Aug 2016	Qaher-1	Najran	hit, 7 civilians killed
19 Aug 2016	R-17E	Khamis Mushayt	confirmed intercept
26 Aug 2016	R-17E	Jizzan Hamiyeh Powerplant	unclear
31 Aug 2016	Zelzal-3	Najran	unclear
2 Sep 2016	Hwasong-6	King Fahd AB	unclear
7 Sep 2016	Burkan-1	unknown	unclear
10 Sep 2016	R-17E	Asir Province	unclear
10 Sep 2016	R-17E	Ash-Shqaiqh Powerplant	confirmed intercept
12 Sep 2016	R-17E	King Khalid AB	confirmed intercept
3 Oct 2016	Qaher-1	Zahran	unclear
4 Oct 2016	Zelzal-3	Camp al-Montazah	unclear
8 Oct 2016	Burkan-1	Khamis Mushayt AB	unclear
9 Oct 2016	Burkan-1	Taif	possible hit; firebrigade and numerous ambulances reported from the area around the base
9 Oct 2016	Burkan-1	Taif	confirmed intercept
20 Oct 2016	Qaher-1	Jizan	unclear
20 Oct 2016	Qaher-1	Najran	unclear
23 Oct 2016	Qaher-2M	Najran, RSBG Base	reportedly scored direct hit
24 Oct 2016	Qaher-2M	Jizan, RSBG Base	reportedly scored direct hit

Date	Missile Type	Target Area	Results
24 Oct 2016	Qaher-2M	unknown	
28 Oct 2016	Burkan-1	Mecca or King Abdul-Aziz International Airport, Jeddah	confirmed intercept 65km from target
1 Nov 2016	Qaher-1	Jazan	unclear
1 Nov 2016	Qaher-1	Najran	unclear
1 Nov 2016	Qaher-1	Asir Province	unclear
8 Nov 2016	Qaher-2M	Ma'rib	confirmed intercept by UAE SA-22
15 Nov 2016	OTR-21	Najran	confirmed intercept
15 Nov 2016	OTR-21	Najran	confirmed intercept
26 Nov 2016	unknown	Khamis Mushayt	confirmed intercept
28 Jan 2017	unknown	Najran	confirmed intercept
31 Jan 2017	Burkan-1	Zuqar Island (Red Sea)	reportedly hit
6 Feb 2017	Burkan-1	Riyadh, Mazhamija Military Base	unclear
22 Feb 2017	Qaher-2M	Mocha	unclear
20 Mar 2017	Burkan/Zelzal-2	Najran	confirmed intercept
14 Apr 2017	12 missiles	Mocha	reportedly intercepted
22 Apr 2017	Qaher-2M	Najran	reportedly hit
27 Jul 2017	Burkan-1	Ta'if/Mecca	confirmed intercept 69km from target
23 Sep 2017	unknown	Khamis Mushayt	confirmed intercept
10 Oct 2017	Qahir-2M	Jizan, Samta Military Base	hit on school in Jizan
29 Oct 2017	Burkan-2H	uinknown	failed on launch from Sa'ada area
4 Nov 2017	Burkan-2H	Riyadh IAP	Reportedly intercepted
1 Dec 2017	Burkan-2H		Missile malfunctioned
30 Nov 2017	Qahir-2M	Khamis Mushayt	confirmed intercept
3 Dec 2017	Claim	Propaganda announcement about a supposed attack on a nuclear reactor under construction in the UAE	this attack did not take place
16 Dec 2017	Qahir-2M	unknown	missile malfunctioned in flight
19 Dec 2017	Burkan-2H	Riyadh	confirmed intercept
19 Dec 2017	Qahir-2M	YNA positions in Jawf	Unclear
26 Dec 2017	Zelzal-2	YNA positions in Nihm	actually S-24 rocket fired in surface-to-surface 'mode'
29 Dec 2017	Qahir-2M	Ma'rib	Unclear
5 Jan 2018	Qahir-2M	Najran	Confirmed intercept
5 Jan 2018	Qahir-2M	Najran	Unclear
12 Jan 2018	Qahir-2M	Najran, RSLF base	Confirmed intercept
13 Jan 2018	Qahir-2M	Unknown	TEL destroyed by RSAF, shortly before launch
17 Jan 2018	Qahir-2M	Unclear	Unclear
18 Jan 2018	Qahir-2M	Jizan	Unclear
23 Jan 2018	Qahir-2M	Unclear	Target was inside Yemen; results of attack remain unclear

A still from a video released by the Saudi MOD, showing a Houthi/Saleh-operated 9P117 TEL shortly before this was destroyed, in October 2016. (MOD of Saudi Arabia)

The Burkan-1 missile as officially announced by the Houthi/Saleh coalition via the al-Masirah TV channel. Apparently, this represented a stretched variant of either the R-17 or Hwasong-6. (al-Masirah TV)

The launch of a Burkan-2H missile in the direction of Riyadh in November 2017. While apparently containing a few spares originating from Iran, this missile represented another R-17 or Hwasong-6 repaired by Yemeni engineers – and not a weapon 'smuggled in' from Iran, as reported by most of the Saudi and US media. With its design being not as advanced as that of the Iranian-made Qiam-1, it also retained small fins, which can be clearly seen on this photograph. (al-Masirah TV)

Launch of a Burkan-1 as shown on a Houthi/Saleh controlled 'Sa'ada News Channel'. (Sa'ada News)

Three Qaher-2M missiles – 'developed' from obsolete V-755-missiles from the S-75 SAMs of Soviet origin. (al-Masirah TV)

The Anti-Ship Force

As well as improvising its Missile Force, the Houthi/Saleh coalition went to great lengths to obtain an anti-ship strike capability. For this purpose, they reached back upon officers and sailors of the former Yemen Navy, including crews of three Chinese-made Type 021 missile boats armed with C.801 anti-ship missiles. The latter were meanwhile destroyed by the Saudi-led coalition of left to rot. But, not so their missiles: Yemeni sailors recovered a number of C.801s and their launchers, installed these on trucks, coupled them with surface-search radars (including Russian-made Cape M1E mobile, coastal radars) and, following several months of testing and training, began deploying these for attacks on the Saudi-led coalition.

The first anti-ship strike was reported on 8 October 2015, around a week after a combined force of Emirati, Bahraini, and Qatari troops forced the Houthi/Saleh coalition to withdraw from the Bab al-Mandab Strait. According to official reports from Sana'a, this attack 'destroyed' the Royal Saudi Navy's tanker *Yunbou*. Two nights later, the Houthi/Saleh coalition struck again, this time reportedly targeting either the Saudi tanker *Boraida*, or an Egyptian warship identified as *al-Mahrousa*. Actually, neither *Boraida*, nor *Yunbou* was even damaged, while *al-Mahrousa* is a 150-year-old presidential yacht that certainly did not venture anywhere near Yemen in years. Nevertheless, the Yemenis kept on trying. On 25 October 2015, they fired a C.801 and claimed a third Saudi warship as 'destroyed', this time releasing a video implying that the ship in question was either a *Baynunah*-class corvette of the United Arab Emirates Navy or the Egyptian Navy's *Oliver Hazard Perry*-class frigate *Taba* (hull number 916). The Houthi/Saleh coalition reported seven further anti-ship attacks in November and December 2015, each time claiming to have sunk a Saudi warship near Bab al-Mandeb. In each instance, the Saudi-led coalition denied any ship was damaged.

Eventually it transpired that in most of the cases in question, no anti-ship missiles were fired, but small boats were used to find and monitor the movement of warships of the Saudi-led coalition underway off the Yemeni coast of the Red Sea. Several times, crews of such boats attempted to attack with RPG-7s – but without success.

Following extensive but fruitless negotiations between Sana'a and Riyadh, and the loss of Bab al-Mandeb, the Houthi/Saleh coalition resumed its anti-ship operations on 1 October 2016. This time, their C.801 missile scored a verifiable direct hit on the catamaran *Swift*, a former US Navy ships leased to the UAE. The missile impacted at the starboard bow and wrecked the ship's bridge, injuring many of the crew but, apparently, killing no one.

In an attempt to support its allies, the USN reacted by deploying two guided-missile destroyers – *USS Mason* (DDG-87) and *USS Nitze* (DDG-94) – supported by the amphibious ship *USS Ponce* (LPD-15) – closer to the Red Sea coast of Yemen.

The Yemenis quickly swallowed the bait and at 19.00hrs local time on 9 October 2016, a missile was fired from the area around the port of Hudaydah. According to USN reports, it crashed into the water several miles away from *USS Mason*, already inside international waters. Another missile struck the sea in the same area around an hour later. Only weeks later did it transpire that *USS Mason* launched two SM-2 SAMs and a single Evolved Sea Sparrow in self-defence, and deployed a Nulka decoy. The USN officially explained that it remains unclear whether any of countermeasures were effective, or the missiles fired by the Houthi/Saleh coalition crashed into the sea on their own. However, in retaliation for such attacks, *USS Nitze* fired several

Since July 2017, the RSAF has deployed its upgraded E-3A RSIP Sentries for operations over Yemen. (RSAF)

Tomahawk cruise missiles on 13 October, and knocked out three radar sites in Houthi territory. Nevertheless, the Houthi/Saleh coalition did launch its third anti-ship strike – this time firing three missiles at *USS San Antonio* (LPD-17) on 15 October 2016. The ship in question was not directly involved in US Navy operations off the Yemeni coast of the Red Sea, but was 'merely passing by', apparently accompanied by *USS Mason*.

This series of attacks ended only after a RSAF air strike on one of the radar stations deployed in the Hudaydah area, a day or two later. Ever since, the Houthi/Saleh coalition fired no further C.801s: whether it had run out of stock, or lost all the radar support for them, remains unclear. This is not to say that the Houthi/Saleh coalition completely stopped all the related effort though. On 26 October 2016, the crew of one of its boats fired an RPG at *SS Teekay*, a 138,000 tonnes ship transporting liquid gas – but missed its giant target.[109]

C.801 missiles taken from fast missile craft of the former Yemeni Navy and deployed in surface-to-sea mode by the Houthi/Saleh coalition – as put on display by the Houthi authorities. (Houthi Release)

An F/A-18D of the Kuwait Air Force, underway 'over southern Arabia' in April 2017. Next to no details have been released about KAF operations in Yemen so far. (Fahd Rihan, via Mohammed Khalid)

An Eurocopter AS.532 U2/A2 Cougar, CSAR helicopter from No. 99 Squadron, RSAF as seen while returning from a sortie over Yemen. (Fahd Rihan, via Mohammed Khalid)

Limited Gains of 2017

Following another failed cease-fire, in November 2016 the Saudi-led coalition launched multiple offensive operations, aiming to expose the Houthi/Saleh coalition to simultaneous pressure on all major frontlines. In the north-west, the YNA advanced on Midi and nearby Haradh. In the south-west, the YNA, Emirati and Sudanese forces launched Operation Golden Spear, aiming to secure the coast of the Red Sea (including the ports of Mocha and Hudaydah), and securing the grip on Ta'izz. In the north-east the Emirati-supported Quietists advanced in the Maslub area (Jawf), while in the south-east the YNA attacked in the Sirwah area.

Many of the air strikes in support of operations in western Yemen were meanwhile flown by UAEAF Mirage 2000s forward deployed at Asseb Airport, in Eritrea. This airfield – dysfunctional since early 1990s – was completely reconstructed by the Emiratis, and housed a detachment of about a dozen Mirages, and several helicopters.[110] Additional support was provided in the form of RJAF F-16s and Sudanese Su-24Ms, the latter of which meanwhile began deploying GPS-assisted guided bombs of Chinese origin. A counterattack by the Houthi/Saleh coalition east of Mocha was quickly crushed and the town surrounded by mid-February 2017. Nevertheless, at sea, their naval service narrowly missed the RSN's frigate *al-Madinah* (FF-702, Type-2000 Class) using a remotely-controlled, semi-submersible explosive boat, on 31 January 2017. On the same day, Mirage fighter-bombers of the UAEAF also destroyed an UAV operated by the Houthi/Saleh coalition shortly before this was launched.[111]

However, the success of most of these operations remained limited – primarily because of continuous instability in southern Yemen, furthered by the activity of AQAP, but also differences between various of the Emirati and Saudi-supported factions. Furthermore, the YNA units involved in these operations suffered heavy losses to mines and ambushes, or became bogged down while fighting for peaks dominating various roads.

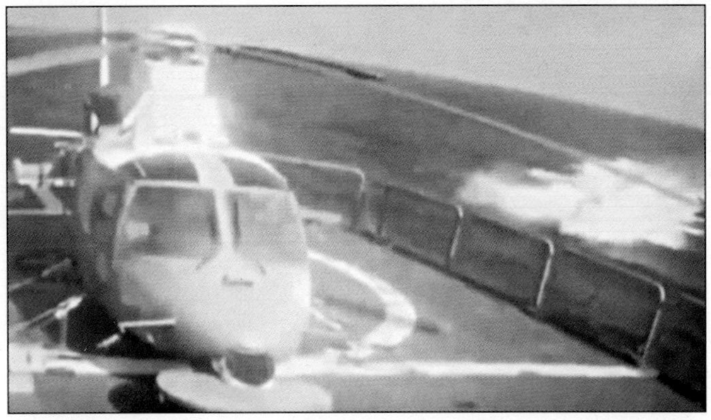

A still from the video taken on board the Royal Saudi Navy's frigate *al-Madinah* when the ship was attacked by a semi-submersible: the wake left by the latter can be seen on the right side. (RSN)

Saleh's Final Coup

The official Saudi aim of the military intervention in Yemen was halting Iranian expansionism and bringing the leaders of the Houthi/Saleh coalition to the negotiating table. Despite the clear failure of nearly two years of negotiations in Kuwait, and although suffering a serious failure in regards of the propaganda war, the Saudi-led coalition largely reached related objectives. However, the Saudis clearly failed to attain their goal of re-establishing a position of influence in Sana'a. In an attempt to break the stalemate, Riyadh thus opened secret negotiations with Saleh. This resulted in the former Yemeni president announcing his split from the Houthis, and the forces under his control attempting to wrestle control over parts of Sana'a in early December 2017. This effort was quickly crushed by the Houthis, and Saleh was killed by a sniper while attempting to flee the capital on 4 December 2017. While this resulted in the defection of several units staffed by Saleh-loyalists from their alliance with the Houthis, it failed to decisively weaken the insurgency: not only that most important military units remained on their side, but the Houthis remained firmly entrenched in Sana'a. The survival of the Hadi government, and that of the Saudi influence in Yemen, thus only became increasingly dependent upon cooperation with the Islah party and affiliated forces.

Royal Saudi Navy's frigate *al-Madinah* returning to the port of Jeddah in January 2017. (RSN)

A Tornado IDS of No. 83 Squadron, RSAF, returning from a reconnaissance sortie over Yemen in mid-2017. (Fahd Rihan, via Mohammed Khalid)

In comparison to the Saudi efforts, the politics pursued by the government of the United Arab Emirates proved much more successful. Indeed, the Emiratis spent most of 2017 securing the Aden area, constructing another forward base (including an airfield) at Perim (or Mayun) Island, and running COIN operations against AQAP in the Mukalla area. Their alliances with the Hirak, the Hadramawt Confederation, the Quietists, and establishment of the Security Belt Forces resulted in the creation of powerful proxies that control nearly all of southern Yemen. In cooperation with these forces, and a mechanised brigade of the Sudanese Defence Forces, the Emiratis continued Operation Golden Spear in the northern direction and – in cooperation with the Sudanese – not only secured the port of Mocha, but also reached positions only 50 kilometres south of Hudaydah in November 2017. A powerful counterattack by the Houthis, launched the next month from the mountains west of Ta'izz with the aim of reaching the coast of the Red Sea and thus cutting off Emirati and allied forces, did cause severe losses to the Hirak and the Sudanese, and slowed down their further advance. However, it also exposed the Houthis and their allies to the vastly superior firepower of their enemies, and resulted in them suffering extensive losses.

Do-It-Yourself Air Defences

Saudi Arabia was thus left without any choice but to once again intensify its war efforts against the Houthis. Following Saleh's death, Riyadh not only offered a bounty for 40 top leaders and allies of the insurgency, but launched an outright man-hunt for them. By mid-January 2018, the Saudi intelligence services and the RSAF tracked down and hit at least five of these.

Greatly weakened and under immense pressure, the Houthis reacted by intensifying their propaganda warfare: they launched a campaign of reporting almost every single air strike by the Saudi-led coalition as causing civilian losses. Simultaneously, the Missile Research and Development Centre and the Missile Force intensified efforts to bolster their air defence capabilities. One of the solutions was to take air-to-air missiles from stocks of the former Yemeni Air Force and attempt deploying them for air-defence purposes. The idea was nothing new: back in 1999, the Serbs adapted Russian-made R-60 (AA-8 Aphid) and R-73 (AA-11 Archer) air-to-air missiles for surface-to-air operations. Yemen acquired a stock of the same missiles back in the 1980s and 1990s, and an even larger number of R-27 (AA-10 Alamo), and R-77 (AA-11 Adder) when buying MiG-29SMs in the 2000s. The challenge was adapting such weapons for deployment from the ground, though without the support of the fire-control systems of the aircraft that are usually carrying them. The latter issue took radar-homing missiles – like R-77 and R-27R – out of the solution: their deployment would require the adaptation of at least one of the N019MP radars and related fire-control systems from MiG-29SMs. Not only was this a complex undertaking, but most of the necessary systems were destroyed early during the war.

Instead, engineers of the Missile Research and Development Centre opted to adapt infra-red homing missiles as SAMs. That effort required the adaptation of APU-60 and P-12 launch rails –

These two releases by the Saudi MOD, from November 2017, contain images taken from FLIR-videos of the RSAF, and document the deployment of R-73 (top) and R-27T air-to-air missiles as makeshift SAMs. (Saudi Ministry of Defence Release)

for the R-60s and R-73s, respectively – on supports mounted on pick-up trucks, together with a reliable supply of electric power and liquid nitrogen to cool their seeker heads.

The first such improvisations were deployed in combat in February 2017, and by June the Houthi-dominated coalition claimed the downing of five fighter-bombers, one helicopter and one UAV. Whether any of the missiles actually scored a hit remains unclear. The reality is that air-to-air missiles are designed to be fired from fast-moving aircraft that are already airborne: thus, their motors are relatively small and light in comparison to the big, heavy, and far more powerful motors of surface-to-air missiles, designed to hurl the missile from the ground and zero speed high into the air. Without such motors, the effective range of air-to-air missiles fired from the ground is dramatically shorter than if they are fired from the air. At least as important is the issue of fire-control: pointing a guided missile in the direction of its target and firing proved insufficient. R-60s and R-73s function better if locked-on at their target before launch. Engineers of the Missile Research and Development Centre found a solution by coupling one of three US-made FLIR Systems ULTRA 8500 turrets – delivered to Yemen back in 2008 – with makeshift controls for their 'new' SAMs. One of these enabled them to fire a R-27T missile that narrowly missed a brand-new Boeing F-15SA from No. 55 Squadron, RSAF, underway over Sana'a, on 7 January 2018. Ironically, while the first related reports only cited the firing of the missile, the Houthi-controlled media in Yemen, and all Iranian media outlets were quick to 'convert' that report into a claim that the targeted F-15 was shot down.

Something similar happened in the case of a Tornado IDS of the RSAF that came down over the northern Sa'ada province on the same day. The aircraft suffered a failure of its oxygen system: this caused a fire inside the cockpit, forcing the crew to eject. Although coming down in an area firmly under Houthi control, both crewmembers were quickly recovered in a combat search and rescue operation run by three SA.532 Cougar helicopters from No. 99 Squadron, supported by eight F-15s and three AH-64s. Nevertheless, the Houthi and Iranian media promptly associated this loss to the deployment of 'new SAMs'. Actually, the missile fired at the F-15SA over Sana'a on 7 January 2018 – was the first ever to get *as close* to its target.

A still from a video released by the Houthi-controlled media, showing a near-miss on an F-15SA from No. 55 Squadron, RSAF, on 7 January 2018, over Sana'a. (Houthi Release)

Saudi Problems and Emirati Success

The war in Yemen has already bolstered Saudi nationalism and rallied the population around the flag, while partially distracting the public attention away from the fact that Crown Prince Mohammad Bin Salman was able to firm his grip on power through a purge of most of the royal family, and thus open the way for far-reaching reforms of his country. On the military plan, this conflict has confirmed the new effectiveness of the Saudi and most of their allied militaries, and – thanks to the constant rotation of units – provided a broad base of combat experience. Obviously, in a country where the public opposition to the government is certain to send one to jail, it's difficult to measure true popular sentiment. However, anti-Iran rhetoric is still running high.

Under such circumstances, the reality about relations between Riyadh, the Houthis and Tehran *de-facto* do not matter and it is little surprising that at the time this is written, the Saudi-led coalition has still failed to provide firm evidence for much-reported 'Iranian support for Houthis' – for example in the form of widely-reported arms deliveries. The handful of ships intercepted by allied warships while supposedly trafficking Iranian arms for Yemen either proved to be crudely constructed ruses, or bound for Somalia, or involved in commercial smuggling enterprises originating in Yemen, not bound for it.[112] Other grossly misreported facts about this war are that the Houthis are neither followers of the Twelver Shi'a, nor of Wilayat al-Faqih ideologies (like the IRGC and the Hezbollah are); that their leadership often acts against Iranian advice, demands and interests; and that at least as many Zaidis are fighting against the Houthis as for them.[113] Instead, the legend is maintained that the Saudi-led intervention in Yemen is a kind of a proxy war against Iran, and a war between the Shi'a and the Sunni.

In the modern-day world, conflicts based on such legends can be continued only for a relatively limited period of time. Unsurprisingly – and despite the fact that the militaries involved on the side of the Saudi-led coalition proved an outright amazing capability to continue intensive combat operations over the years – every additional day of the war in Yemen is making it ever more clear, that there is no *military* solution for all the conflicts it includes. Reasons for this include not only diametrically oppositional interests of various of foreign powers of a political and commercial nature. Diverse strongmen inside Yemen have quickly learned how to profit thanks to the war: from their point of few, it is only of advantage if much of the country, its economy and infrastructure are destroyed, hundreds of thousands displaced, and nearly 70% of the population are living on the brink of the famine.

Table 6: Claimed and Confirmed Attrition of the Coalition Aircraft, Helicopters & UAVs, 2015-2017 (confirmed entries in bold print)

Date	Air Force/ Unit	Aircraft Type	Notes
26 Mar 2015	RSAF	'3 aircraft'	claimed shot down by Houthi/Saleh coalition during opening air strikes on Sana'a and Sa'ada; no evidence provided
26 Mar 2015	UAEAF	'1 aircraft'	claimed shot down by Houthi/Saleh coalition when UAE announced its participation in Operation Decisive Storm; no evidence provided
26 Mar 2015	RSLF	'helicopter'	claimed shot down by Houthi/Saleh coalition near the border to Saudi Arabia; no evidence provided
27 Mar 2015	**RSAF**	**F-15S**	**claimed shot down by Houthi/Saleh coalition; reportedly lost due to technical malfunction; crew recovered from the Red Sea by US special forces**
27 Mar 2015	SuAF	Su-24M	claimed shot down by Houthi/Saleh coalition; no evidence provided
7 May 2015	RSLF	AH-64A	claimed shot down by Houthi/Saleh coalition in Najran area; no evidence provided
10 May 2015	**FRA**	**F-16C**	**serial 08-8008; shot down by ground fire in Wadi Nashour area, Sa'ada Province; pilot 1st Lt Bathi KIA**
20 May 2015	RSLF	AH-64	claimed shot down by Houthi/Saleh coalition in Najran area; no evidence provided
23 May 2015	RSAF	F-15S	forced to jettison ordnance in emergency; possibly damaged
24 May 2015	RSAF	'1 aircraft'	claimed shot down by Houthi/Saleh coalition in Sa'ada area; no evidence provided
25 May 2015	RSAF	'1 aircraft'	claimed shot down by Houthi/Saleh coalition over al-Malil, Kitaf district; no evidence provided
4 Aug 2015	**RSLF**	**AH-64A**	**hit by ground fire; made emergency landing inside Saudi Arabia; crew of two lightly injured**
21 Aug 2015	**RSLF**	**AH-64A**	**claimed shot down by Houthi/Saleh coalition; crew killed; official cause 'technical malfunction'**
26 Aug 2015	**UAEAF**	**Camcopter S-100**	**shot down by Houthi/Saleh coalition in Mukayris area**
26 Aug 2015	**RSLF**	**UAV**	**shot down by Houthi/Saleh coalition near the border to Saudi Arabia**
3 Sep 2015	**RSLF**	**Micro-UAV**	**shot down by Houthi/Saleh coalition in Sa'ada area**
13 Sep 2015	UAEAF	AH-64	claimed shot down by 'anti-aircraft missile' over Horaib, Ma'rib province; no evidence provided
26 Sep 2015	RBAF	Helicopter	claimed shot down by Houthi/Saleh coalition in Ma'rib area; crew of five reportedly killed, but no evidence provided
15 Oct 2015	RSAF	'Saudi F-16'	claimed shot down by Houthi/Saleh coalition; pilot reportedly captured but no evidence provided
21 Oct 2015	**RSAF**	**F-15S**	**crashed on landing at Khamis Mushayt AB, causing multiple secondaries; reason for the loss and fate of crew unknown**
25 Oct 2015	**UAEAF**	**UAV**	**shot down by Houthi/Saleh coalition over Ta'izz, photographs of wreckage released**
27 Oct 2015	unknown	'transport aircraft'	claimed shot down by Houthi/Saleh coalition over Ta'izz; no evidence provided
12 Dec 2015	UAEAF	F-16	claimed as damaged by Houthi/Saleh coalition; reportedly crashed on landing at Anad AB; no evidence provided
30 Dec 2015	**RBAF**	**F-16C**	**claimed shot down by Houthi/Saleh coalition; crashed in Fifa mountains, Jizan**
?? Dec 2015	RSAF	F-15S	crashed on landing at Khamis Mushayt AB, causing multiple secondaries
8 Jan 2016	RSLF	AH-64	claimed shot down by Houthi/Saleh coalition; no evidence provided
20 Jan 2016	RSAF	'Saudi F-15'	claimed shot down by SA-2 SAM-site operated by Houthi/Saleh coalition
20 Jan 2016	**UAEAF**	**UAV**	**claimed shot down by SA-2 SAM-site operated by Houthi/Saleh coalition**
13 Mar 2016	**UAEAF**	**Mirage 2000-9D**	**claimed shot down by the AQAP, Aden; crew of two killed**
26 Sep 2016	**RSAF**	**WD-1 Wing Loong**	**UAV, Khulan, Sana'a**
30 Dec 2016	**RSLF**	**AH-64D**	**Najran, claimed shot down by Houthi/Saleh coalition; circumstances unclear but loss confirmed**
30 Jan 2017	**RSNF**	**SA.365F**	**Hudaydah, reportedly crashed due to technical malfunction; crew recovered**
24 Feb 2017	**RJAF**	**F-16AM**	**Najran, crashed, pilot recovered**
18 Apr 2017	**RSLF**	**UH-60**	**crashed in Ma'rib area, 12 of crew and passengers killed**
21 May 2017	RSAF	F-15	claimed shot down by Houthi/Saleh coalition over Sana'a; no evidence provided
8 Jun 2017	RSAF	F-15	claimed shot down by Houthi/Saleh coalition over Sana'a; no evidence provided

Date	Air Force/ Unit	Aircraft Type	Notes
10 Jun 2017	RSAF	'Saudi F-16'	claimed shot down by Houthi/Saleh coalition; no evidence provided
10 Jun 2017	**RSAF**	**CH-4**	**confirmed shot down over northern Yemen**
11 Aug 2017	**UAEAF**	**UH-60M**	**crashed in the Shabwa area; four occupants killed**
11 Sep 2017	**UAEAF**	**AT-802**	**crashed in the Red Sea; pilot killed, WSO injured**
14 Sep 2017	**RSAF**	**EF-2000**	**reportedly crashed due to technical malfunction during CAS against AQAP; pilot killed**
1 Oct 2017	**USA**	**MQ-9**	**shot down by SA-9 over Sana'a**
16 Oct 2017	**UAEAF**	**AH-64**	**crashed in southern Yemen; crew of two killed**
28 Oct 2017	RSAF	EF-2000	Claimed shot down by Houthi/Saleh coalition over northern Yemen; no evidence provided
7 Jan 2018	**RSAF**	**Tornado IDS**	**malfunction of oxygen system caused a fire inside the cockpit; crew ejected over northern Sa'ada province and recovered by helicopters of No. 99 Squadron RSAF**
7 Jan 2018	**RSAF**	**F-15SA**	**damaged by R-27T while underway over Sana'a (claimed shot down by Houthi-led coalition); repaired at as-Sala'am Works**
22 Mar 2018	**RSAF**	**F-15S**	**damaged by R-27T; repaired at as-Sala'am Works**

Troops of the 14th Armoured Brigade YNA, with Emirati Prince Sattam Bin Hathloul, on a battlefield in southern Yemen in April 2017. (UAE MOD)

Armed with two Paveway IV laser-homing bombs, this EF-2000 from No. 80 Squadron, RSAF, was photographed at dawn over Yemen. The type was recently involved in operations against AQAP in the Mukalla area too. (Fahd Rihan, via Mohammed Khalid)

Intensity of operations over Yemen during the first two years of the war was such that many RSAF fighter-bombers wear markings for 110 and more sorties flown. (Fahd Rihan, via Mohammed Khalid)

BIBLIOGRAPHY

Barany, Z., *The Challenges of Building a National Army in Yemen*, (CSIS, July 2016)

Carapico, S., *Arabia Incognita: Dispatches from Yemen and the Gulf* (Charlottesville: Just World Books, 2016, ISBN 9781682570036)

Curtis, M., *Unpeople: Britain's Secret Human Right Abuses* (London: Vintage Books, 2004, ISBN 978-00994696728)

Day, S., *Regionalism and Rebellion in Yemen: A Troubled National Union* (Cambridge: Cambridge University Press, 2012, ISBN 978-1107606593)

Dresch, P., *A History of Modern Yemen* (Cambridge: Cambridge University Press, 2010, ISBN 0-521-79482X)

Ginny, H., *Yemen Endures: Civil War, Saudi Adventurism and The Future of Arabia* (London: Hurst, 2017, ISBN 9781849048057)

Gordon, S., 'Abyani Tribes and al-Qaeda in the Arabian Peninsula in Yemen', (*Criticalthreats.org*, 25 July 2012)

Hart-Davis, D., *The War That Never Was: The True Story of the Men Who Fought Britain's Most Secret Battle*, (London, Century, 2011, ISBN 9781846058257)

Heinze, Marie-Christine (Editor), *Yemen and the Search for Stability: Power, Politics and Society After the Arab Spring* (London: I. B. Tauris Publishers, 2017, ISBN 9781784534653)

Perkins, Brian M, 'The Risks of Forgetting Yemen's Southern Secessionist Movement', *WarOnTheRocks.com*, (13 March 2017)

Perkins, Brian M., 'Yemen: Between Revolution and Regression', *Studies in Conflict & Terrorism*, Volume 40, 2017 – Issue 4

Perry, M., 'US Generals: Saudi Intervention in Yemen "a bad Idea"', *al-Jazeera America*, (17 April 2015)

Salamani, B. A., Loidolt, B. & Wells, M., *Regime and Periphery in Northern Yemen; the Huthi Phenomenon*, (RAND, 2010; DS247. Y48S236 2010)

Schmidt, D. A., *Yemen: The Unknown War* (London, The Bodley Head Ltd. 1968, ISBN 370-00411-6)

Stafrace, C., *Arab Air Forces* (Carrollton, Squadron/Signal Publications Inc., ISBN 0-89747-326-4)

UN Security Council, *Letter dated 27 January 2017 from the Panel of Experts on Yemen addressed to the President of the Security Council*, UNSC, 31 January 2017

Interviews with various Egyptian, Iraqi, Saudi, and Yemeni air force officers, pilots, and ground personnel (see Acknowledgments and Endnotes)

NOTES

1 Oleg Teterin, *In Egypt and in Zanzibar: Memoires of Soviet Military Translators, 1960-1966* (Memories Publishing, 2011; in Russian).

2 For further discussion of related topics, see Cooper et all, *Arab MiGs Volumes 2 & 3*, where extensive excerpts from relevant parts of the 'Document 44' (the latter contains official findings of investigation into the reasons for catastrophic defeat during the June 1967 Arab-Israeli War).

3 'Hosni Mubarak: President of the Arab Republic of Egypt', *TASS*, 27 May 2004; 'Mubarak's Aircraft: President of Egypt was Befriended to Ryazan Pilots', *Mala Rodina*, 24 October 2014; Ferris, p.97.

4 Teterin, as cited above.

5 The process of bi-annual Egyptian-Soviet negotiations is described in great detail in *Arab MiGs Volume 2*.

6 Charles Schmitz, 'Ironic Zaydis in Yemen', *TheMaydan.com*, 19 October 2016.

7 Day, pp.89-93.

8 Youssef Aboul-Enein, 'The Egyptian-Yemen War (1962-1967): Egyptian Perspectives on Guerrilla Warfare', *Infantry Magazine*, January-February 2004.

9 Curtis, pp.288-290.

10 Dresch, pp.31-32.

11 Ibid & M. T. L., interview provided on condition of anonymity, September 2004.

12 Baer, p.133.

13 A. A., interview provided on condition of anonymity, October 2013.

14 Tom Cooper & Thomas Newdick, 'Fitter Sunset', *Combat Aircraft magazine*, July 2016.

15 'President of Yemen to Visit Russian Aircraft Building Corporation MiG', *Praym-Tass*, 18 December 2002; 'Russia delivers MiG-29 warplanes to Yemen', *Interfax-AVN*, 11 July 2002; 'Yemen to Buy Six More MiG-29s', *ITAR-TASS*, 19 December 2002 & Piotr Butwoski, *Russia's Warplanes, Volume 1* (Houston, Harpia Publishing, 2015), ISBN 978-0-9854554-5-3, pp.18-20. Known serials of the YAF MiG-29s range from 22-01 to 22-35.

16 Jack Serle, 'Yemen's Barely Functional Air Force Points to US Involvement in Strikes', *The Bureau of Investigative Journalism*, 29 March, 2012.

17 Georg Mader, 'The Situation in Yemen – An Air Force Assessment', *Military Technology*, 30 March 2015. Notable is that – contrary to Russian advertisements, but exactly as in the case of other customers for this system, including Algeria, Syria and Venezuela – the upgrade of SA-3s to Pechora-2M standard included no 'full digitalisation' of the existing system. This proved impossible because the system has been out of production for decades. Instead, the Russian companies involved took over and overhauled stocks of associated radars, missiles, and launchers of the Russian Air-Space Force, installed these on wheeled vehicles, and mated them with a command post equipped with digital computers and displays only. A. N. interview provided on condition of anonymity, October 2015.

18 David E Sanger & Thom Shanker, 'Threats and Responses: Reluctant US Gives Assent for Missiles to Go to Yemen', *New York Times*, 12 December 2002. The Hwasong-6 is essentially a slightly stretched Scud, with a downsized warhead but enlarged fuel tanks, which nearly double the range in comparison to the original missile. The 'interruption' in question was caused by an interception of Cambodia-registered merchant *So San*, in December 2002, while this ship was carrying 15 missiles with conventional, high-explosive warheads and 23 tanks of nitric acid.

19 A. K. H., interview provided on condition of anonymity, January 2011 & S. H., interview provided on condition of anonymity, July 2011. Unless otherwise stated, backgrounds for the

following two sub-chapters are based on transcriptions of these two interviews.

20 'War on Sa'ada – Analysis', *YemenOline*, 24 July 2008.

21 Cable 09SANAA2186_a, 'Who are the Houthis, Part Two: How Are They Fighting?', US Embassy in Sana'a, 9 December 2009 (https://wikileaks.org/plusd/cables/09SANAA2186_a.html). Unless otherwise stated, most of this sub-chapter is based on information from that cable.

22 Nicole Stracke, 'Counter-Terrorism and Weapons Smuggling: Success and Failure of Yemeni-Saudi Colaboration', *Gulf Research Center Security and Terrorism Research Bulletin*, Issue 4, November 2006 & N. N., interview provided on condition of anonymity. Questioned about the reasons for the government's failure to prevent Yemeni arms dealers from selling arms to Houthis, the source explained the situation as follows:
'The government imposed a ban on carrying weapons in major cities, and then a ban on selling specific weapons on local markets. Cut off from their usual customers, many dealers were left without a choice but to sell to Houthis. The more arms they sold to Houthis, the more demand there was; and the more demand there were from Houthis, the more interesting this business became even for military officers allied with Saleh.'

23 N. N., interview provided on condition of anonymity, citing 'Abd al-Malik al-Houthi: La Nurahin a'ala Ayy Quwwa Iqlimiya wa Idha Awqafat as-Sulta Istihdafna, Sanana-tahi at-Tamtarus'.

24 'Two MiG-29s Downed in Yemen', *MENL*, 13 March 2007.

25 Mohammed Sudan, 'Yemen Reiterates Ceasefire Conditions for Rebels', *Reuters*, 21 August 2009 & Nasser Arabyee, 'Ending the Conflict', *al-Ahram*, 22 August 2009.

26 Zaid al-Alaya'a & Nasser Arabyee, 'Two al-Houthi Field Leaders Killed', *Yemen Observer*, 24 August 2004 & 'Yemen Troops Kill Leader, Dozens Dead', *Reuters*, 17 August 2009.

27 'Yemen Says Air Force Kills Rebel Leader', *Reuters*, 30 August 2009; 'Yemeni Army Kills Scores in Sa'ada', *al-Jazeera*, 22 September 2009; 'Yemen Army Air Raid Kills 80 Civilians: Witnesses', *al-Arabiya.net*, 17 September 2009; 'Hundreds of Rebels Killed in North Yemen', *UPI*, & 'State-Run Media: Yemeni Military Kills 150 rebels', *CNN*, 21 September 2009.

28 'Yemen: Iran's Role in an Intensifying Insurgency', *STRATFOR*, 7 October 2009; Adam Rawnsley, 'Iran-Backed Terror Group Parades New Anti-Aircraft Missiles in Iraq', *WarIsBoring*, 19 March 2015; Cable: 09SANAA2186, 9 December 2009, *Wikileaks*.

29 'Yemeni Fighter Planes Shot Down by Hezbollah's Elements', *YemenPost*, 11 October 2009.

30 N. N., interview provided on condition of anonymity, April 2010; this and most of subsequent quotations from the same source are based on transcription of the same interview.

31 Nasser Arabyee, 'Continuous Confrontations Between al-Houthi Rebels and Saudi Forces Kill Dozens', *YemenObserver*, 5 November 2009 & 'Saudis Push Back Yemen Rebels', *BBC*, 8 November 2009.

32 N. B., interview provided on condition of anonymity, November 2010. Notable is that despite dozens of such reports about the involvement of the Islamic Revolutionary Guards Corps (IRGC) of Iran, or of the Hezbollah from Lebanon on the Houthi side in period 2004-2010 – published foremost by Saudi, but also Israeli and US sources – no firm evidence for such deployments in Yemen was ever published before 2015.

33 'Yemen: 2 Houthi commanders killed in north', PressTV, 18 November 2009; 'Saudi Troops Killed in Yemen Rebel Clashes', *Reuters*, 22 November 2009; 'Saudi Forces Fighting in Yemen', al-Jazeera, 24 November 2009; 'Saudis Claim Key Mountain Win over Yemeni Rebels', *Khaleej Times*, 29 November 2009.

34 '7 civilians killed in Saudi blitz in northern Yemen', PressTV, 25 January 2010 & 'Yemen rebels announce truce with Saudi Arabia', al-Arabiya, 25 January 2010; 'Yemen Rebels Leave Saudi-Arabia', al-Jazeera, 25 January 2010 & 'Yemen Houthi Rebels quit stronghold in Sa'ada', *al-Arabiya*, 25 February 2010. By that point in time, official Saudi sources confirmed a loss of 113 soldiers killed.

35 A. A., interview provided on condition of anonymity, October 2013; *Yemen Country Study, Volume 1: Strategic Information and Developments* (Washington, International Business Publications, 2013); Jeremy Scahill, 'The Dangerous US Game in Yemen', *The Nation*, 18 April 2011 & Jeremy M Sharp, Yemen: Background and US Relations, *Congressional Research Service*, 11 February 2015. Notable is that on 27 March 2007 a US UAV was shot down by a YAF MiG-29, but then hurriedly declared as 'belonging to Iran' (see 'Yemen shoots down foreign drone', *Reuters*, 28 March 2007).

36 Brian Dodwell and Marielle Ness, 'A View from the CT Foxhole: an Interview with Captain Robert A Newson, Military Fellow, Council on Foreign Relations', *Combating Terrorism Center at West Point* (ctc.usma.edu), 27 February 2015.

37 Ahmed al-Haj, 'Yemen air force jet bombs bus by mistake; 4 dead', *Reuters*, 29 June 2011 & 'More than 40 dead in south Yemen violence', *AP*, 1 July 2011; 'Civilians killed in Yemen air attack', *al-Jazeera*, 5 September 2011; 'Al-Qaeda in Yemen vows to avenge southern air raids', *Arab News*, 14 September 2011; 'Sana'a: 280 kill in al-Qaeda fight', *MENA*, 14 September 2011.

38 'Yemen air force commander killed in car bomb attack', *Reuters*, 12 October 2011; 'Al-Qaeda's air war in Yemen', *Khaleej Times*, 22 May 2013; 'Yemen gunmen kill air force officer', *Yemen National*, 1 June 2013; 'Bomb tears through Yemen air force bus, killing officer', *Reuters*, 25 August 2013; 'Two Yemeni air force colonels killed in less than 24 hours', *Yemen Times*, 25 September 2013; 'Qaeda suspects kill Yemen air force pilot', *AFP*, 13 February 2015. Notable is that US military instructors deployed in Yemen before 2015 repeatedly stressed the Houthi eagerness to fight – and to defeat AQAP, see Brian Dodwell & Marielle Ness, 'A View from the CT Foxhole: an Interview with Captain Robert A Newson, Military Fellow, Council on Foreign Relations', ctc.usma.edu, 2015.

39 M. T. L., interview provided on condition of anonymity, September 2004; A. A., interview provided on condition of anonymity, October 2013 & various reports in the Yemeni and international media.

40 Sharon Weinberger, 'Yemen's Arab Spring Leaves Its Air Force in Disarray', *AW&ST*, 19 March 2012 & Jack Serle, 'Yemen's Barely Functional Air Force Points to US Involvement in Strikes', *The Bureau of Investigative Journalism*, 29 March, 2012; 'Presidential Appointment Decree for Command Positions in the Armed Forces', SABA, 10 April 2013; 'Firefight exchange at Headquarters of 27th Mechanised Brigade in Mukalla', *Aden al-Ghad*, 4 June 2013; 'Yemeni Officer survives Assassination Attempt', *CNN*, 18 August 2012; 'At-Tahiri Commander of the IV Military District and ash-Shami and Muhsen Assistants to Political Security', *26 September News,* 2 January 2015; 'Commander of the Naval Forces and Commander of the IV Military District visit Mayun Island', *Yemen Now*, 14 August 2014; 'Minister of Defence Assesses Readiness of 17th Infantry and 170th Air Defence Brigades in Ta'izz', *26 September News*,

12 October 2014; 'End of Military Training Flights in Anad Air Base', *Marib Press*, 1 April 2013; 'Presidential Decree Dividing the Theatre of Military Operations in the Republic of Yemen, Designating Military Districts and Appointing Commanders', *SABA*, 10 April 2013; 'New Commanders Appointed in Air and Air Defence', *Yemen Press*, 6 December 2014; 'Commander of V Military District Inspects Situation in Rabaia'a Base', *Yemen Press*, 14 September 2014.

41 'Soldiers From the 3rd Mountain Brigade Leave Ma'rib after Plundering Weapons and Supplies', *Marib Press*, 22 May 2013; 'Armed Confrontations in the 3rd Mountain Brigade and Expulsion of Brigade's Chief of Operations and Sale of Weapons on the Black Market', *Marib Press*, 4 February 2013; 'Forces of Dissolved Division Begin to Leave the Capital and Re-Deploy in Three Governorates', *Sahafah*, 25 June 2013; 'President of Yemen to Visit Russian Aircraft Building Corporation MiG', *Praym-Tass*, 18 December 2002; Volodymyr Guzenko (who served as an instructor in Yemen at the time), 'Black News From Yemen', *Borysfen Intel*, 9 December 2013 & 'Presidential Decrees Appointing Officers in Posts in Armed Forces', *SABA*, 13 July 2014. According to unconfirmed reports, the SS-1s were operated by the 4th, and OTR-21s by the 5th Brigade MBG, but their precise allocation became irrelevant in the light of subsequent developments.

42 'New Commanders Appointed in Air and Air Defence', Yemen Press, 6 December 2014; 'Air Force Commander meets with Deputy Commander of Special Operations for CENTCOM', SABA, 16 June 2014.

43 M. T. L., interview provided on condition of anonymity, September 2004; A. A., interview provided on condition of anonymity, October 2013 & various reports in the Yemeni and international media.

44 'Yemeni air force bombs rebels after ceasefire collapses', *WordBulletin*, 5 July 2014.

45 Charles Schmitz, 'The Fall of Amran and the Future of the Islah Party in Yemen', *Middle East Institute*, 25 August 2014; Adel Moujahed al-Shrhabi, 'Houthi Victory is defeat for Yemen's Islah', *al-Monitor*, 29 September 2014; 'Rebels push into Yemen's capital Sanaa', *al-Akhbar* (English), 18 September 2014. Subsequent developments were to show that – contrary to early reports – the Houthis did not 'destroy' the 310th Armoured Brigade, but only blocked it. The unit was subsequently withdrawn to southern Yemen, and re-organized. See below for further details.

46 'Three Sukhois Delivered to Houthi-Controlled Port in Yemen', *Jane's*, 19 February 2015.

47 Marie-Christine Heinze, 'The Crisis in Yemen – The primacy of stability over real change', *Qantara.de*, 20 January 2015.

48 'Zakaria ash-Shami is the Deputy Chief of Staff', *Yemen24.com*, 28. December 2014; 'Yemeni President accuses Houthis of coup attempt', *al-Akhbar*, 20 September 2014; 'Yemen's Ballistic Missiles in Houthi Hands', *AP*, 21 January 2015; 'Yemen Crisis: President Resigns as Rebels tighten hold', *BBC*, 22 January 2015; 'Houthi Rebels Take Over Yemen's Government', *The Huffington Post*, 6 February 2015.

49 al-Araby al-Jadeed, 'Houthis take partial control of Yemeni Air Force', *al-Araby.co.uk*, 22 February 2015; 'Gulf States say will not let Yemen become Terrorism Hub', *al-Arabiya News*, 18 March 2015 & Farea al-Muslimi, 'Yemen Air Fore Falls into Grip of Houthis', *al-Monitor*, 29 April 2015.

50 UN Security Council, *Letter dated 27 January 2017 from the Panel of Experts on Yemen addressed to the President of the Security Council*, UNSC, 31 January 2017 (henceforth: 'Letter'), p.22. According to most of Western observers, the National Security Bureau, established in 2002 to counter the influence of Wahhabi-Islamists and sympathisers in the Political Security Organization. Until 2012, it was commanded by Ammar Muhammad Abdullah Saleh – another of Saleh's nephews.

51 Perkins, 'Yemen', pp.301-317.

52 Haykal Bafana, 'Hadhramaut: Rebellion, Federalism or Independence in Yemen?', *Muftah.org*, 22 April 2014.

53 'Targeting Saada: Unlawful Coalition Airstrikes on Saada City in Yemen', *HRW*, 30 June 2015.

54 al-Araby al-Jadeed, 'Houthis take partial control of Yemeni Air Force', *al-Araby.co.uk*, 22 February 2015; 'Gulf States say will not let Yemen become Terrorism Hub', *al-Arabiya News*, 18 March 2015 & Farea al-Muslimi, 'Yemen Air Fore Falls into Grip of Houthis', *al-Monitor*, 29 April 2015. According to available reports, it was this series of decisions that caused such widespread disagreement within the YAF, that most of its personnel left their positions and – literally – disappeared.

55 Based upon the few interviews conducted with former Yemen Army officers (all provided on condition of anonymity), opposition to any kind of foreign intervention was influential in the decision to side with the Houthi/Saleh coalition. Others blamed Hadi for not doing enough against AQAP. Finally, Hadi constrained the activities and decision-making of military commanders, while the Houthis encouraged them to act on their own initiative. Many of the Yemeni officers proved themselves as more skilled, and were much more successful, if acting in accordance with what is generally known, in the West, as the *Auftragstaktik*, they thus preferred to serve under the Houthi/Saleh command.

56 This table is based on nearly 250 different media reports, primarily of Yemeni origin and published in Arabic: while some of these are mentioned elsewhere around this book, most have been left out for reasons of space. Notable for most of the reports in question is that they were rarely – if ever – denied by the other parties involved in this conflict: indeed, with the exception of fewer than a handful of cases (mentioned elsewhere), it seems that there is little dispute over what commanders and what units joined what side in this war.

57 'Al-Subaihi Captured and Lahij Falls as Houthis move on Aden', *Yemen Times*, 25 March 2015 & 'Yemen's President Hadi Flees Houthi Rebel Advance on Aden', *AP*, 25 March 2015.

58 'Yemen's Hadi withdraws resignations, as UN pushes for dialogue', *Middle East Eye*, 24 February 2015; 'Yemen's President Hadi asks UN to back intervention', *BBC*, 25 March 2015.

59 'Yemen anti-Hadi officer escapes assassination', *Arab Today*, 20 March 2015.

60 Hamza Hendawi, 'Warplanes Bomb Presidential Palace in Yemen's Aden', *The Huffington Post*, 20 March 2015; Khalid al-Karimi, 'Southerners Prepare for Houthi Invasion', *Yemen Times*, 23 March 2015 and similar reports.

61 'Yemen's Ansurallah fighters enter port of Mocha, two towns in south, *Iran Daily*, 24 March 2015; 'Saudi Coalition Hits Houthi Stronghold as Aden Battle Rages', *Bloomberg*, 31 March 2015; Notably, the 33rd Armoured Brigade was entirely staffed by the Shafi.

62 'Yemen's Port of Aden under Threat with Enemy at the Gates', *Reuters*, 27 March 2015; 'Heavy fighting in Yemen's Aden as Houthis Approach from the East', *Irish Times*, 30 March 2015; 'Warships shell Houthis outside Yemeni City of Aden', *Reuters*, 30 March 2015; 'Saudi Coalition Hits Houthi Stronghold as Aden Battle Rages', *Bloomberg*, 31 March 2015.

63 K. A. S., interview provided on condition of anonymity, May 2017 & Dr. Michael Knights, 'The Saudi-UAE War Effort in Yemen (Part 2): The Air Campaign', The Washington Institute for Near East Policy (washingtoninstitute.org), 11 August, 2015.
64 K. A. S. interview provided on condition of anonymity, May 2017.
65 Ibid.
66 S. E., former military advisor in Saudi Arabia, interview provided on condition of anonymity, April-May 2015.
67 Notably, while official, the designations 'Typhoon FGR.Mk 50' (single-seaters) and 'Typhoon T.Mk 51' seem not to be used in practice.
68 Rajiv Chandrasekaran, 'In the UAE, the United States has a quiet, potent ally nicknamed 'Little Sparta'", *Washington Post*, 9 November 2014.
69 A. A., interview provided on condition of anonymity, March 2015; 'Decisive Storm Destroys Houthi Missile Stockpile', *al-Arabiya* (English), 28 March 2015; 'The Houthi are launching ballistic missile in the direction of the Kingdom of Saudi Arabia!', *al-Arabiya* (in Arabic), 29 March 2015
70 Despite countless reports about air strikes on Yemeni air bases, as of September 2017, only the destruction of following YAF aircraft and helicopters has been visually confirmed: 1 AB.412, 1 CN.235M, 1 F-5B and 1 F-5E, 2 Il-76, 1 Mi-8, 3 MiG-21bis, 2 MiG-29, 4 Su-22, 1 UH-1H, and 1 Z-142.
71 S. P., interview provided on condition of anonymity, September 2009; K. A. S. interview provided on condition of anonymity, May 2017; 'Saudi Pilots Detail Typhoon's Progress', *Flightglobal.com*, 11 July 2011; 'Saudi Typhoons Use Paveway IV Bombs on ISIS', *DefenseNews.com*, 1 March 2015.
72 'Pro-Houthi Brigade disintegrates in Yemen ad-Dali', Word Bulletin, 1 April 2015 & ,Yemen's pro-government forces retake city from Shite rebels', *The Record*, 26 May 2015.
73 K. A. S. interview provided on condition of anonymity, May 2017.
74 'Op Decisive Storm ends in Yemen', *al-Arabiya* (English), 21 April 2015.
75 'Military reinforcements cross Saudi border to Yemen', *MiddleEastMonitor.com*, 7 August 2015; 'Coalition Forces Hit Yemeni Rebels, advance towards Capital Sana'a', *AFP*, 29 August 2015; Dylan Vosman, 'HIMARS Artillery Rocket System of UAE heading to Ma'rib, Yemen', Defence-blog.com, 30 August 2015.
76 See related reporting by al-Jazeera, BBC, WAM and other news agencies. The UAE acquired up to 50 Pantsir-S1 systems from Russia starting in 2005, and as a part of a deal to curb Russian arms export to Iran. In Yemen, the Emiratis deployed the wheeled variant, mounted on the MAN SX45 truck – the only Western vehicle said to be able to accommodate the S1 system.
77 Dr. Michael Knights, 'The Saudi-UAE War Effort in Yemen (Part 2): The Air Campaign', The Washington Institute for Near East Policy (washingtoninstitute.org), 11 August, 2015.
78 'Saudi-led air strikes target Houthi bastion in Yemen's Sa'ada province', Globe and Mail, 7 May 2015.
79 'Yemen: Saudi-Led Airstrikes Used Cluster Munitions', *HRW*, 3 May 2015. According to the same report, Textron completed deliveries of 1,000 CBU-105 Sensor Fused Weapons for the UAEAF in December 2010, and then concluded a contract for delivery of 1,300 CBU-105s to Saudi Arabia as late as of August 2013; and 'US: Stop Providing Cluster Munitions'; 2 June 2016.
80 Angus McDowall, Phil Stewart, David Rohde, 'Yemen's Guerrilla War Tests Military Ambitions of big-spending Saudis', *Reuters*, 19 April 2016. Notable is that in comparison, the UN investigation found evidence of at least 38 violations of international humanitarian law by the Houthi/Saleh coalition.
81 'Targeting Saada: Unlawful Coalition Airstrikes on Saada City in Yemen', *HRW*, 30 June 2015; '2571 Civilians Killed, 3897 Wounded by Coalition Strikes', Yemen Observer, 14 April 2015; '4,903 civilians killed, nearly 11,300 children injured', *Yemen Post*, 11 September 2015.
82 'US trying to restrain Saudi Arabia on deadly Yemen airstrikes', *Los Angeles Times*, 21 April 2015; 'Saudi-Led Coalition in Yemen Relied Heavily on US Intelligence', *Washington Post*, 27 March 2015; Angus McDowall, Phil Stewart, David Rohde, 'Yemen's Guerrilla War Tests Military Ambitions of big-spending Saudis', *Reuters*, 19 April 2016.
83 'Saudi Snoops: RSAF Turns to King Airs', *Defenseindustrydaily.com*, 25 August 2014.
84 'US Launches Aerial Refuelling Mission in Yemen', *DefenseNews.com*, 8 April 2015.
85 Hakim Almasmari, 'Yemenis turn Against Saudi-led Bombing', *The Wall Street Journal*, 1 April 2015.
86 Zaid al-Alayaa, 'Airstrikes hit wedding in Yemen; as many as 135 dead', *Los Angeles Times*, 28 September 2015 & 'Second Yemen Wedding bombed as UN says Houthi rebels accept cease-fire', *The Guardian*, 8 October 2015.
87 'Yemen: Saudi-Led Airstrikes Used Cluster Munitions', *HRW*, 3 May 2015. According to the same report, Textron completed deliveries of 1,000 CBU-105 Sensor Fused Weapons for the UAEAF in December 2010, and then concluded a contract for delivery of 1,300 CBU-105s to Saudi Arabia as late as of August 2013; and 'US: Stop Providing Cluster Munitions'; 2 June 2016.
88 'Yemen: Events of 2016', HRW, 25 February 2017; Unaware of reality, the Houthis cheerfully claimed to have shot down a number of Saudi-operated mini-UAVs early during the war.
89 'Fighting Party Destroys Yemeni-Saudi Border Crossing – Witness', *The Peninsula*, 24 May 2015.
90 'Air Strikes kill at least 80 in deadliest bombings of Yemen War', *Reuters*, 28 May 2015.
91 A. K. H., interview provided on condition of anonymity.
92 'Commander of Saudi Brigade Martyred in Cross-Border Attack from Yemen', *KUNA*, 24 August 2015.
93 'Report: Saudi-Led Airstrikes Kill 25 Civilians in Yemen', VOANews.com, 27 September 2015.
94 Not all such operations proved successful. Only four days later, a group of Saudi special forces was completely destroyed by Houthis near a place named Bakhawih, in northern Yemen.
95 'Explosions rip through Homes in Yemen's Capital after Air Strikes', *New York Times*, 21 April 2015 & 'US trying to restrain Saudi Arabia on deadly Yemen airstrikes', *Los Angeles Times*, 21 April 2015.
96 '80 Missiles Hit Saudi Border Guard Headquarters in Jizan', *FNA*, 24 May 2015.
97 'Yemen Crisis: Saudi Arabia shoots down Scud missile', *BBC*, 6 June 2015; 'How Saudi Arabia Shot down Scud Missile Fired from Yemen', *Christian Science Monitor.com*, 6 June 2015 & 'Scud Missiles fired into Saudi Arabia from Yemen traced to North Korea: Official', Koreaherald.com, 29 July 2015.
98 'Saudi Arabia Armed Forces intercept, destroy Scud-type Ballistic Missile fired from Yemen', *WAM*, 27 August 2015.
99 Reports about results of the R-17E attack on Khamis Mushayt on 15 October 2015 vary widely. Some Yemenis are stressing the missile flew in the wrong direction and exploded in the air high above Hudaydah; reports from Saudi Arabia indicate either an

interception short of or a hit in the vicinity of Khamis Mushayt AB. On the contrary, the Iranian media (FNA, 16 October 2015) reported the death of '66 high-ranking Saudi officers and commanders', and destruction of '17 F-15 fighter jets and 9 Apache helicopters'.

100 'China to Open First Drone Factory in Saudi Arabia', *UPI*, 29 March 2017; the factory in question was opened at the King Abdul Aziz City for Science and Technology. As well as pressing Chinese-made UAVs into service, in November 2015, Saudi Arabia signed a major contract aimed to replenish depleted ammunition stocks of the RSAF. According to the Defense Security Cooperation Agency (*News Release, Transmittal No. 15-57*, 16 November 2015), this included orders for 1000 GBU-10 Paveway II kits and 2,300 BU-117/Mk.84 bombs, 4020 Paveway II kits and 8020 BLU-111/Mk.82 bombs, 1100 GBU-24 Paveway III kits and 1500 BLU-109 penetrator warheads, 400 KMU-556 kits for GBU-31/V1 Joint Direct Attack Munitions (JDAM), 1000 KMU-557 kits for GBU-31(V3) JDAMs, 3000 KMU-572 kits for GBU-38 JDAMs, 2000 GBU-48 Enhanced Paveway II (dual mode GPS and laser guided bombs), 2000 BLU-110/Mk.83 bombs, 500 KMU-572 kits for GBU-54 and 300 KMU-556 kits for GBU-56 guided bombs.

101 Rick Gladstone, 'Airstrikes Kill Dozens of Civilians in Yemen, Doctors Without Borders Says', *New York Times*, 21 August 2015.

102 Michael Safi & Joshua Robertson, 'An Australian Mercenary has reportedly been killed in clashes in Yemen, alongside six Colombian Troops', *The Guardian*, 9 December 2015.

103 In a report issued by the FNA on the same morning – and forwarded by numerous other media outlets around the world without any cross-examination – 'two OTR-21s' caused the death of 146 Saudi-led troops, and the destruction of three AH-64s. A closer examination, with the help of first-hand sources in the area, provided no evidence for any kind of a missile strike, and subsequently the details of the assassination also became known.

104 According to official Saudi sources, cited in the foreign media, over 400 civilians had been killed or injured in missile attacks by the Houthi/Saleh Coalition. Similar sources cited foreign diplomats that added that up to 400 Saudi soldiers and border guards were killed in the course of battles along the border by early 2017.

105 Saeed al-Batati, 'Tip-offs helped Accelerate al-Mukalla Liberation', *Gulf News*, 9 May 2016 & Hassan Hassan, 'UAE shows the way to deal with regional crises', *The National*, 3 July 2016.

106 M. K. F., interview provided on condition of anonymity, August 2017 & 'Saudi Arabia Shoots Down 11 Scuds, Deploys Patriots to Counter Ballistic Missiles Fired from Yemeni Rebels', *DefenseWorld.net*, 26 November 2016.

107 'Houthi Forces appear to be using Iranian-made drones to ram Saudi air defences in Yemen, report says', *Washington Post*, 22 March 2017.

108 'Arab Coalition destroys Houthi Missile Launch Site in Yemen's Hudaydah', *al-Arabiya*, 12 October 2017.

109 'RPG fired at gas ship off Yemen', *Splash247.com*, 26 October 2016.

110 'UAE deploys Fast Jets to Eritrea', *Jane's Defence Weekly*, 14 November 2016. Ever since, the UAEAF has regularly rotated detachments of fighter-bombers to Asseb, and used the local port as a starting point for operations against the Houthi/Saleh coalition along the Red Sea coast.

111 'UAE protests Iran's arming Yemen rebels with drones', AFP, 2 February 2017.

112 'Letter dated 12 July 2013 from the Chair of the Security Council Committee pursuant to resolutions 751 (1992) and 1907 (2009) concerning Somalia and Eritrea addressed to the President of the Security Council', United Nations, Security Council, 12 July 2013; 'Letter dated 1 June 2015 from the Panel of Experts established pursuant to Security Council resolution 1929 (2010) addressed to the President of the Security Council', *United Nations, Security Council*, 2 June 2015 & Cable 09SANAA2186_a, 'Who are the Houthis, Part Two: How Are They Fighting?', US Embassy in Sana'a, 9 December 2009 (https://wikileaks.org/plusd/cables/09SANAA2186_a.html).

113 Ali Watkins, Ryan Grim & Akbar Shahid Ahmed: 'Iran Warned Houthis Against Yemen Takeover', *HuffingtonPost.com*, 20 April 2015 & 'Houthi Leader Slams Iranian Chief-of-Staff', *MiddleEastMonitor.com*, 28 November 2016.

ABOUT THIS BOOK

Since September 1962, hardly a week has passed without a major armed confrontation or an outright war in Yemen. The number of long-lasting insurgencies, mutinies, rebellions, or terrorism-related activities that took place during this period goes into the dozens. Despite the duration of all these conflicts and although they may have caused as many as half a million deaths, the rest of the World has heard very little about them. At best, Yemen is nowadays known as a hotbed of international terrorism, an area that is on the receiving end of frequent US air strikes flown by UAVs, or as 'some place' fiercely bombarded by a coalition led by Saudi Arabia.

While at least some details about British operations in what was Southern Arabia of the 1960s were published over the years, next to nothing is known about activities of local air forces. This is even more surprising considering that for nearly two decades there were no less than two, fully developed services of that kind – one operated by what was then North Yemen, another by what used to be South Yemen – and that these were also deeply involved in the Cold War.

Using newly released secret intelligence sources, neglected memoirs, and popular memory, this book tells the story of military flying in Yemen since 1962. It is provides in-depth insight and analysis of the campaigns fought by the Egyptian air force of the 1960s, the creation of two Yemeni air forces in the 1970s, an entire series of inter-Yemeni wars of the 1980s and 1990s, and the wars since 2000 that ultimately resulted in the collapse of the country and its military in 2015. Containing over 140 photographs, colour profiles, maps and extensive tables, Hot Skies over Yemen is a richly illustrated and unique point of reference about one segment of modern aerial warfare that remains largely unknown until today.

TOM COOPER

Tom Cooper is an Austrian aerial warfare analyst and historian. Following a career in worldwide transportation business – during which he established a network of contacts in the Middle East and Africa – he moved into narrow-focus analysis and writing on small, little-known air forces and conflicts, about which he has collected extensive archives. That resulted in specialisation in such Middle Eastern air forces as of those of Egypt, Iran, Iraq, and Syria, plus various African and Asian air forces. Except for authoring and co-authoring more than 30 books – including an in-depth analysis of major Arab air forces at wars with Israel in period 1955-1973 – and over 1000 articles, Cooper is a regular correspondent for multiple official defence-related publications.